INSTANT PROGRAMS

FOR YOUTH GROUPS

1

From the Editors of Group Publishing

Group Books

Loveland, Colorado

LIST OF CONTRIBUTORS

Ambrose, Dub
Anderson, Joan
Beach, Barbara
Becker, Dennis
Benson, Dennis
Carvalho, John
Clifford, Pam
Eskew, Lane

Fuller, Marty
Goto, Dawn
Guttierrez, Milton
Hansen, Cindy
Huff, Anna
Kaiser, Eldor
Korth, Dawn
Parolini, Cindy

Pickle, Kimberly
Roehlkepartain, Jolene
Schultz, Joani
Schultz, Thom
Sharpton, Ben
Shaw, Nancy M.
Sparks, Lee
Stewart, Ed

Instant Programs for Youth Groups 1
Copyright © 1988 by Thom Schultz Publications, Inc.

Third Printing, 1990

Credits
Designed by Judy Atwood
Illustrations by Jan Aufdemberge, RoseAnne Buerge, Jan Knudson, Laurel Finnerty and Michael Streff

Scripture quotations are from the Holy Bible, New International Version. Copyright © 1973, 1978, 1984 International Bible Society. Used by permission of Zondervan Bible Publishers.

Library of Congress Cataloging-in-Publication Data
Instant programs for youth groups: from the editors of Group Publishing.
    p.   cm.
  ISBN 0-931529-32-8 (soft: v. 1)
  1. Church group work with youth. 2. Church group work with young adults.
  I. Group Publishing.
BV4447.I495 1988
259'.2—dc19   87-36874

Printed in the United States of America

CONTENTS

INTRODUCTION

"What am I going to do with the youth group this week?"

"How can I find creative activities to do with my group?"

"How can I plan unique experiences for my kids with a minimal amount of preparation?"

In response to many youth leaders' requests for help, Group Publishing's editors have compiled this resource. *Instant Programs for Youth Groups 1* offers a multitude of creative yet meaningful activities—all combined into one handy resource. The meetings require minimal preparation. They include step-by-step instructions on what to do and how to do it. They also offer quality handouts that are ready to copy, a great help for busy youth leaders.

This resource includes practical, proven programs from GROUP Magazine's "How to Use GROUP Members Only" regular feature, plus expanded and adapted articles from GROUP Members Only. The programs concentrate on the needs and concerns faced by today's young people. Program topics include shyness, self-image, birth order, drinking, pressures, job stress, hardship, competition, leadership, hypocrisy, church, faith sharing, missions, complaining, rock music and AIDS.

As you use these timely programs, watch your young people grow in their relationships with God and others. Notice how they interact in discussions and respond to the involvement activities. Watch your young people develop a personal faith that will be the basis for a mature adult faith. Exploring and questioning faith issues within a supportive environment allows your young people the chance to see God at work in themselves, others and the world.

So open the book. Pick a topic. Get ready for an exciting meeting. And be prepared to experience God at work in your life and the lives of your young people as you use this special resource, *Instant Programs for Youth Groups 1*.

SECTION ONE:

Self-Image

1. SHY STUFF

Purpose:
To help group members uncover the topic of shyness.

Session outline:

1. Standing ovations—Gather the group members in a circle. Have two volunteers leave the room while the rest of the group thinks of a "pose" for this pair. For example, a pose could be each standing on one leg and holding hands. Make sure the pose isn't too complicated. When the volunteers come back, they must try to guess the pose by doing different poses. They know they're getting close to the right pose because the group applauds when the pose is almost correct. When they hit upon the correct pose, the group gives them a standing ovation. Play this game several times so different pairs have a chance to get a standing ovation.

Materials:
☐ newsprint
☐ markers
☐ posterboard
☐ copies of handouts
☐ Bibles
☐ pencils

2. "A Shyness Inventory"—Talk about the game. Ask: "Did you ever feel shy about participating in the game? If so, when? Did the standing ovations help overcome shyness? Why or why not? What else helps overcome shyness?"

Have individuals complete and discuss the handout "A Shyness Inventory."

3. Reasons for shyness—Dr. Arden Watson, professor of speech communications at the University of Rhode Island at Kingston, identifies three reasons for shyness:
● Fear of rejection.
● Linking a harmless situation with a fearful one.
● Lack of skills.
On newsprint, write the reasons for shyness as you talk about them.

Say: "There are three reasons for shyness. First, fear of rejection. A person will shy away from others to avoid being rejected. Second, linking a harmless situation with a fearful one. For example, you might avoid all parties because no one asked you to dance at a sixth-grade party. Third, lack of skills. You linger quietly by the door because you don't know how to mingle.

"Which reason do you most identify with in your bouts with shyness? What are some ways you can begin to conquer shyness in these areas?" Write kids' responses on the newsprint.

4. "Shy Symptoms"—Have kids complete the "Shy Symptoms" handout and share the results in small groups.

5. "Shymometer"—Create a giant "Shymometer" (like the one on the handout) with posterboard and markers. Make a movable arrow on it. Have kids do the written exercise on the "Shymometer" handout. When kids tell about their situations, have them explain by using the posterboard "Shymometer."

6. Celebrate your gifts—Move the group into a large circle. Place one chair in the center. Have each group member take a turn sitting in the center chair. As one person sits silently in the center, invite other group members to tell him or her the skills, talents, abilities and traits they admire. Have someone write down all the comments on a "We Celebrate Your Gifts" handout and present it to the individual to take home. Repeat the process with every group member.

7. Celebrate your Creator—Divide the verses of Psalm 139:1-16 among group members. Have the individuals or small groups create newsprint posters to symbolize the verses assigned. Have a young person slowly read aloud the passage while kids display their posters. Hang the Psalm on the youth room wall or somewhere in the church.

KEEP GOING!

A Shyness Inventory

Think of 10 people you know. Write their names in the following blanks.

1. _____
2. _____
3. _____
4. _____
5. _____
6. _____
7. _____
8. _____
9. _____
10. _____

Chances are:
- eight of these people admit they're now shy or have been shy at some point in their lives.
- the other two people have felt shy in certain settings, though they wouldn't label themselves as shy.
- three people in your list consider themselves shy now.
- four of these people often feel anxious in small group situations.

Shy Symptoms

Study the following list of "shy symptoms." Circle the ones that describe what happens when you feel shy.

When I feel shy, I . . .

blush
cling to the wall
tell jokes
act cool

space out
tremble
eat a lot
develop "butterflies"
  in my stomach

clam up
feel embarrassed
stutter
act bashful

get sweaty palms
get sweaty underarms
get a sweaty forehead
get a sweaty upper lip

act crazy
laugh and giggle a lot
put down others around me
lose eye contact with people

Shymometer

Read the following situations. Circle the appropriate number on the meter on the left to indicate how shy you feel in each situation. A "1" indicates you're not shy at all. A "5" indicates a great deal of shyness. Next circle the number on the meter on the right to indicate how you'd like to respond.

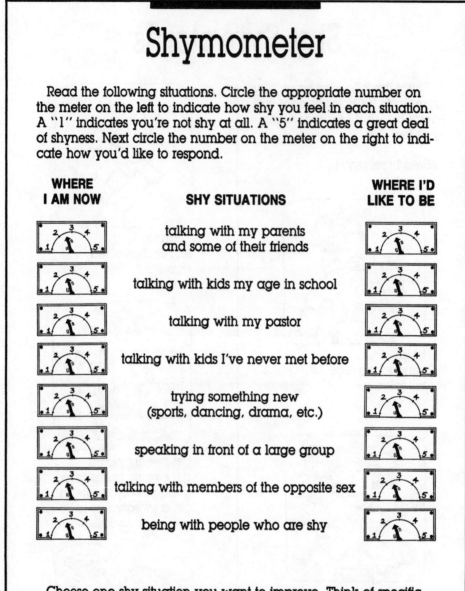

WHERE I AM NOW	SHY SITUATIONS	WHERE I'D LIKE TO BE
	talking with my parents and some of their friends	
	talking with kids my age in school	
	talking with my pastor	
	talking with kids I've never met before	
	trying something new (sports, dancing, drama, etc.)	
	speaking in front of a large group	
	talking with members of the opposite sex	
	being with people who are shy	

Choose one shy situation you want to improve. Think of specific ways you can get where you'd like to be. Then put them into action!

We Celebrate Your Gifts

Fill out this sheet for each group member as he or she sits in the center of the room and receives comments from the group. Give the person the sheet at the end of his or her turn.

We see and admire these qualities in

_____

(group member's name)

2. HI, I'M UGLY

Purpose:

To help group members accept themselves.

Session outline:

1. Attribute appreciation—As group members enter, have them write their names on 3×5 cards and give the cards to you. After everyone has arrived, mix up the cards and give each person a card that has someone else's name on it. Have group members each write on the card three physical attributes they admire about the person whose name is on the card. Collect the cards for later use.

Materials:
- ☐ 3×5 cards
- ☐ two pair of full-body long johns
- ☐ about 50 deflated balloons
- ☐ gingerbread-man figures
- ☐ gingerbread cookies
- ☐ copies of handouts
- ☐ Bibles
- ☐ pencils
- ☐ straight pins

2. Create a muscleman—Divide the group into two teams. Give each team a large pair of full-body long johns. The smallest team member wears the long johns over his or her clothes.

Throw about 50 deflated balloons into the center of the room. Each team will blow up as many balloons as it can and stuff them into the long johns in five minutes. Count the balloons by popping them with a straight pin while the team counts out loud.

3. "Body Stereotypes"—Give each kid a copy of the "Body Stereotypes" handout. Have kids complete the activity on the handout and share their answers in small groups of four to six. Distribute copies of the "No Laughing Matter" handout. Have small groups read the true story about a girl who said her figure nixed her chance to be a cheerleader. Discuss the questions.

In the large group ask: "Do you need certain physical characteristics to be a cheerleader? Why or why not? What other activities require certain 'bodies' (for example, football, gymnastics, ballet)? Is it 'bad' that some activities work best if a person has a certain physique? Explain. Should people be restricted from certain activities because of their physical appearance? Why or why not?''

4. Body language—Give each group member a pencil and a paper gingerbread-man figure. Have group members each mark three areas on the paper figure to represent three things they wish they could change about their physical appearance.

Move kids back into small groups. Have group members display their paper figures and share what they wish they could change about their bodies and why.

5. Physical statements—Read the following statements to the large group. Invite kids to make one of the following responses to each statement you read: those who disagree with the statement should remain seated; those who moderately agree should stand up; those who rabidly agree should stand, applaud and cheer.

● A real secret for personal appearance is to accept ourselves with all our imperfections.

● Almost all teenagers have looked in the mirror and wondered what it would cost for a face transplant.

● It would be great if all teenagers looked like fashion-magazine models.

● Your body is like your personality—it's unique, one of a kind, a gift from God.

● An appearance that some would label ''ugly'' may be just what you need to keep you humble in a world that often worships beauty.

● Learning to laugh at yourself not only helps you, it helps the people around you.

● Your unique appearance isn't something to be ashamed of, it's something to celebrate.

6. Accentuating the positive—Take out the 3×5 cards you collected earlier. One at a time, read the three positive qualities written on each card, and allow group members to guess who the card is written about. After they guess, give the card to that group member.

7. Closing—For refreshments, serve the gingerbread cookies.

Body Stereotypes

Write what abilities you associate with each of the following body types. Tell why.

1. Is it wrong to stereotype bodies and abilities? Why or why not?

2. Read 1 Corinthians 3:16-17; 6:19-20. If God doesn't judge by appearances, why does he call our bodies "temples"? Does it matter how people look if their bodies portray the Holy Spirit? Explain.

No Laughing Matter

Read the following true story about a girl who said her figure nixed her chances to be a cheerleader. Discuss the following questions with your group.

People often joke about large breasts. But it was no laughing matter when a California high school senior was told she didn't make the cheerleading squad because her breasts were too large.

The senior, Sandy,* filed a $1 million lawsuit against her school district after a teacher allegedly told the teenager her grades and performance were acceptable, but her figure wasn't.

"What upset me was that my daughter believed this," Sandy's mother said at a news conference. "She thought her body was wrong. She was embarrassed. She just wanted to die."

The school principal said Sandy's skills were what kept her from making the squad—not her physical appearance.

*Name has been changed.

Discuss It

1. How would you feel if you were Sandy? her mother? her teacher? her principal?

2. Should Sandy have made the cheerleading squad? Why or why not?

3. Was Sandy right to file a lawsuit? Why or why not? What if she really wasn't skilled enough?

4. Read 1 Samuel 16:7 and Galatians 2:6. What do these verses say about judging appearances? How do they apply to Sandy? to how you view your school's cheerleaders? to your view of your own body? What's most important to God?

5. How would you help Sandy feel better about herself if you were her best friend?

3. MIRROR, MIRROR ON THE WALL

Purpose:
To help group members accept their looks.

Session outline:

1. Mirror, mirror—Hang a mirror for kids to look in as they arrive. Tape a sign on the mirror that says, "You're looking at one special person."

2. Commercials—Divide the group into groups of four to six. Have the groups make up and act out "bad" commercials; tell kids to focus on bad things commercials say about people's looks such as bad breath, body odor, split ends, zits or being overweight. Discuss how commercials influence people's actions and attitudes.

3. Three-way mirror—Draw a large three-way mirror on newsprint. Label the three sections: "God," "Self" and "Media." Ask kids to write words and phrases telling how they think God's mirror, their own mirror and the media's mirror reflect them. For example, a kid might write "forgiven" under "God," "trying" under "Self," and "never good enough" under "Media."

4. Following the ads—Form small groups. Distribute women's and body-building magazines. Have each small group look through the magazines for weight-control, body-building or beauty products. Tear out a few ads from the magazines. Have group members discuss:

● What do these ads teach about body image?

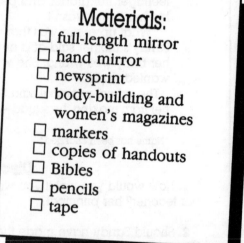

Materials:
☐ full-length mirror
☐ hand mirror
☐ newsprint
☐ body-building and women's magazines
☐ markers
☐ copies of handouts
☐ Bibles
☐ pencils
☐ tape

● How do you feel when you see these ads?

● If you could change part of yourself to look like the people in these ads, what would you change?

5. "Looking at Your Looks"—Get kids all together. Pass out copies of the "Looking at Your Looks" handout and have everyone complete and score it individually. Ask, "How do you feel about your physical appearance?"

6. "The Fat Quiz"—Read "The Fat Quiz" aloud to help your group understand important facts about body weight, health and dieting. As you read each statement, have kids guess which answer fits in each blank. (The answers are: 18, 15, 8, 10, 15, 95, 39, northeast, west, 55, 33.)

7. Rewrite the ads—Have each small group make and present an ad proclaiming what God would say about our bodies. Compare the groups' ads with real ads. Ask: "What's the media's message? What's God's message?"

Choose a volunteer to read Luke 12:22-29. Ask: "What three things do you celebrate about your body? What one thing would you like to change? Is it changeable? If not, how can you accept it? If so, what realistic goal can you set to change it?"

8. You're okay—Provide newsprint and markers. Ask small groups to trace an outline of each person. Ask each small group member to complete this sentence under each outline: "I like you, (name), just the way you are because . . ." Have each kid keep his or her own picture.

Say: "If dieting and body building don't change how you see yourself in the mirror, what can you do? You can change mirrors. One reason you don't like what you see in the media's mirror is because that mirror is distorted. It doesn't reflect who you really are. A much better mirror is God's mirror. It reflects a person God formed in his image. So it shows you as you really are.

"Luke 12:22-29 challenges you to have faith. And that faith includes not worrying about your body, clothes or food. Instead, it means letting go of those obsessions. It means learning to trust the God who loves you and meets your needs. And as you learn to trust God, you'll begin to see the same beauty in yourself that God gave to the lilies of the field.

"So look at yourself in God's mirror. And smile. See that child of God who's loved and accepted despite heavy hips or sagging biceps. You're a beautiful person. And God loves you just the way you are."

9. Prayer—For a closing prayer, form a circle. Pass around a mirror and have each group member look into the mirror and complete, "Mirror, mirror, on the wall, thanks, God, for my _____ most of all."

Looking at Your Looks

Take this quick test to see how you feel about your looks. Read each statement. Then circle the number that best represents how much you agree with the statement (1=strongly agree; 5=strongly disagree). Be honest. Circle how you feel, not how you think you should feel.

Statements	Strongly agree				Strongly disagree
	1	2	3	4	5
I wish I was better-looking.	1	2	3	4	5
If I built up my body, the opposite sex would find me more attractive.	1	2	3	4	5
I'd die without a summer tan.	1	2	3	4	5
I wish I could start an exercise routine.	1	2	3	4	5
I need to eat more nutritious foods.	1	2	3	4	5
I wear nice clothes to feel good about myself.	1	2	3	4	5
Whenever I pass a mirror, I always notice how I look.	1	2	3	4	5
I worry about getting fat.	1	2	3	4	5
I feel pressured to look my best all the time.	1	2	3	4	5
I'm embarrassed about how I look in a swimsuit.	1	2	3	4	5
I need to lose (or gain) more weight.	1	2	3	4	5
I feel it's important to look attractive.	1	2	3	4	5
Before going out, I spend a lot of time getting ready.	1	2	3	4	5
I'm always changing fashions and hair styles to improve my looks.	1	2	3	4	5
				Total:	

When you finish, add the numbers you circled. If you scored 36 or below, you're uptight about your body. You spend a lot of time trying to look better. Think of ways to spend less time in front of the mirror and more time feeling good about yourself.

If you scored 37 to 47, congratulations. You have a balanced view of your body. You think your body's important. But you don't spend all your time taking care of it.

If you scored 48 or above, you're avoiding your body. You may feel embarrassed about your looks. Or you may think looks aren't important. Spend a little more time taking care of your body so you can feel better about yourself.

The Fat Quiz

Answer the following questions. Choose from the list of answers. Note: Beware! A few extra answers have been added to make it tough.

8	15	39
10	18	55
15	33	95
lobotomy	face lift	south
northeast	west	east

1. By the time you're 17, you will have spent _____ months looking in a mirror.

2. As many as _____ percent of teenage girls suffer from bulimia or anorexia.

3. One out of _____ 10th-graders tries to lose weight by vomiting, taking laxatives or using drugs.

4. The average person goes on a diet _____ times a year.

5. The diet industry is a _____ billion dollar a year business.

6. Do diets work? Of people who diet, _____ percent gain back the weight they lose.

7. Obesity rose _____ percent between 1963 and 1980 for 12- to 17-year-olds.

8. The fattest teenagers live in the _____.

9. The skinniest teenagers live in the _____.

10. _____ percent of teenage girls feel "terrified" of becoming fat.

11. Nearly _____ percent of white teenage guys were overweight in their preteen years.

4. CLUES TO YOUR PERSONALITY

Purpose:

To help group members understand how their birth order affects their personality.

Session outline:

1. Let's have a party—Have group members decorate the meeting room for a birthday party. Provide birthday-party hats, balloons, banners, plates, cups and napkins.

2. Birthday-party games—Have group members lead birthday-party games like Pin the Tail on the Donkey and Musical Chairs. Give each person birthday candles to represent his or her birth-order position. Give one candle to kids who are the oldest child in their family, two candles to second-oldest kids, and so on. Have the kids hold the candles until later in the meeting.

3. Family trees—Give everyone several paper leaves and a marker. Have each kid write the name of every family member, including self, on a separate leaf. Ask kids to tape their leaf-names in order of birth to a piece of string hanging from a large tree branch you have brought into the room.

Ask a volunteer to read 2 Corinthians 5:17. Say, "No matter how many are in your family or whether you are first, middle or last in the family tree, you are a special, unique creation in God's sight."

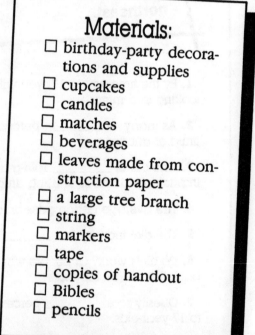

Materials:
- [ ] birthday-party decorations and supplies
- [ ] cupcakes
- [ ] candles
- [ ] matches
- [ ] beverages
- [ ] leaves made from construction paper
- [ ] a large tree branch
- [ ] string
- [ ] markers
- [ ] tape
- [ ] copies of handout
- [ ] Bibles
- [ ] pencils

4. "Discover Who You Are"—Distribute copies of the handout. Have group members take the quiz individually as directed.

5. Birth order cheers—Divide the group into small groups according to birth order with no more than six kids in a group. Have kids who are oldest in their family go to one corner, and so on. Ask small groups to share their answers to the "Discover Who You Are" quiz. Have small groups discuss these questions:

● What do I need to be careful about because of my birth order?

● What strengths come from my birth order?

Have each group prepare and present an energetic cheer based on the qualities of their birth order.

6. Relationships—Move kids into new small groups with every member of each group having a different birth order. Again, no more than six kids in a group. Have the groups discuss these questions:

● What do I like about my birth order?

● What bugs me about my birth order?

● What are the birth orders of my mother and father?

● How does birth order influence how we relate to other family members?

7. Take the cake—Give each person a cupcake. Have the group members each place their candles on their cupcake and light the candles. Sing "Happy Birthday" (with each person using his or her own name). Divide the group into pairs. Have one person in each pair blow out his or her candles while the other person says a prayer of thanksgiving for him or her. Then have the second person blow out his or her candles while the first person says a prayer of thanksgiving.

Read Philippians 1:6 to the group. Say: "God made each person special when he or she was born. He'll continue to treat each guy and girl as a special person."

Discover Who You Are

Take this quiz to see how closely your personality traits match those of others with your same birth order. First, circle your birth order. Then go down each of the four columns, checkmarking the characteristics you feel best describe you. When you're done, look back at each of the columns. Did you mostly checkmark the characteristics common to people with your birth order? Or did you checkmark traits that are more common to another birth order? How do you explain the similarities? the differences?

I am . . .

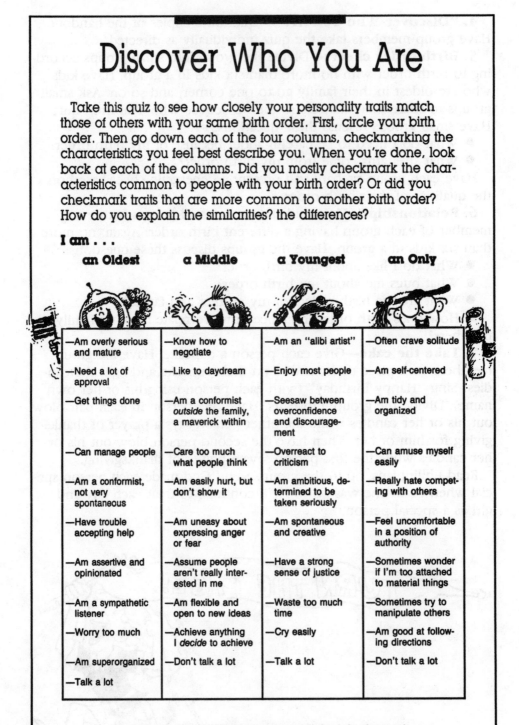

an Oldest	a Middle	a Youngest	an Only
—Am overly serious and mature	—Know how to negotiate	—Am an "alibi artist"	—Often crave solitude
—Need a lot of approval	—Like to daydream	—Enjoy most people	—Am self-centered
—Get things done	—Am a conformist *outside* the family, a maverick within	—Seesaw between overconfidence and discouragement	—Am tidy and organized
—Can manage people	—Care too much what people think	—Overreact to criticism	—Can amuse myself easily
—Am a conformist, not very spontaneous	—Am easily hurt, but don't show it	—Am ambitious, determined to be taken seriously	—Really hate competing with others
—Have trouble accepting help	—Am uneasy about expressing anger or fear	—Am spontaneous and creative	—Feel uncomfortable in a position of authority
—Am assertive and opinionated	—Assume people aren't really interested in me	—Have a strong sense of justice	—Sometimes wonder if I'm too attached to material things
—Am a sympathetic listener	—Am flexible and open to new ideas	—Waste too much time	—Sometimes try to manipulate others
—Worry too much	—Achieve anything I *decide* to achieve	—Cry easily	—Am good at following directions
—Am superorganized	—Don't talk a lot	—Talk a lot	—Don't talk a lot
—Talk a lot			

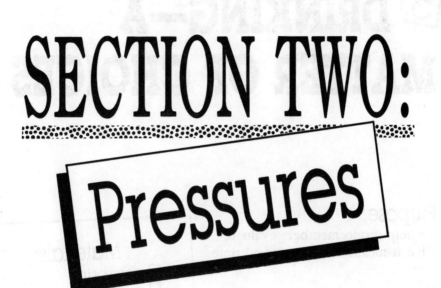

SECTION TWO:

Pressures

5. DRINKING—A MATTER OF CHOICES

Purpose:

To help group members evaluate what it means to have a good time.

Session outline:

1. Getting ready—Ask four to eight young people to prepare the skit, "A Teenager Drinks Himself to Death."

Ask three young people to work together to create a list of 10 words commonly associated with a "good time." For example, use words like food, friends, party or music. Ask them to set up a hidden microphone and a tape recorder for use during the meeting.

Materials:
- [ ] newsprint
- [ ] marker
- [ ] props for skit
- [ ] copies of handouts
- [ ] pencils
- [ ] Bibles
- [ ] audio tape
- [ ] tape recorder and microphone

2. "Good time" gauge—Begin the meeting by explaining that you want to check what members consider to be a good time. Tell them you'll use their applause as a measuring tool.

Have one young person read the list and pause for applause after each word. Have another person secretly record the applause. After all 10 words have been read and applauded, play back the tape and time each reaction.

On newsprint, list the three items that had the longest applause. Talk about these items. Ask:
- Were the items serious or silly? Explain.
- What items would you add to the list?
- How would the list be different if your classmates rated it? your parents?

● When does a desire to have a good time get in the way or become dangerous?

3. A skit—Set the stage by explaining that this skit is based on a true story of young people who were having a "good time."

4. "What I Learned From Another's Experience"—Distribute the handout and have kids respond individually to the questions about drinking. Divide group members into four small groups to discuss the questions under "What did I learn?"

5. "What Does the Bible Say?"—Make copies of the handout and assign a Bible study to each of the four small groups. Encourage kids to discuss the questions and share their discussions with the other groups.

6. Special guest—If possible, invite a reformed alcoholic to speak to your group. Ask the person to briefly focus on what he or she used to consider a good time and how or why that's different now. Allow time for questions and answers.

7. Blessings for the good times—Prerecord a closing devotional thought: Ask one or two young people to read Ephesians 3:16-21 for the spoken portion. Use music as background for the reading, like "Grace," an instrumental on the flip side of "We Are the World" (Columbia Records).

NEXT PAGE!

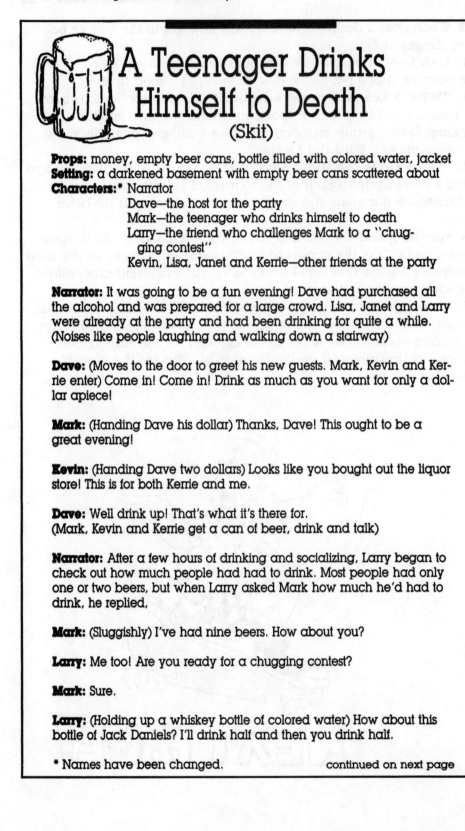

A Teenager Drinks Himself to Death
(Skit)

Props: money, empty beer cans, bottle filled with colored water, jacket
Setting: a darkened basement with empty beer cans scattered about
Characters:* Narrator
      Dave—the host for the party
      Mark—the teenager who drinks himself to death
      Larry—the friend who challenges Mark to a "chug-
        ging contest"
      Kevin, Lisa, Janet and Kerrie—other friends at the party

Narrator: It was going to be a fun evening! Dave had purchased all the alcohol and was prepared for a large crowd. Lisa, Janet and Larry were already at the party and had been drinking for quite a while. (Noises like people laughing and walking down a stairway)

Dave: (Moves to the door to greet his new guests. Mark, Kevin and Kerrie enter) Come in! Come in! Drink as much as you want for only a dollar apiece!

Mark: (Handing Dave his dollar) Thanks, Dave! This ought to be a great evening!

Kevin: (Handing Dave two dollars) Looks like you bought out the liquor store! This is for both Kerrie and me.

Dave: Well drink up! That's what it's there for.
(Mark, Kevin and Kerrie get a can of beer, drink and talk)

Narrator: After a few hours of drinking and socializing, Larry began to check out how much people had had to drink. Most people had only one or two beers, but when Larry asked Mark how much he'd had to drink, he replied,

Mark: (Sluggishly) I've had nine beers. How about you?

Larry: Me too! Are you ready for a chugging contest?

Mark: Sure.

Larry: (Holding up a whiskey bottle of colored water) How about this bottle of Jack Daniels? I'll drink half and then you drink half.

---

* Names have been changed. continued on next page

Mark: (In a sarcastic slur) If you think you can do it.
(Larry takes the bottle, opens it and proceeds to swallow half the bottle without stopping. Mark stops Larry when he reaches the halfway point, wipes off the mouth of the bottle with his shirt sleeve and chugs the rest without stopping. By this time everyone in the group is watching and cheering both guys' accomplishments. When Mark finishes, Dave checks with both guys in the contest)

Dave: I think you guys are drinking too much.

Mark: (Slowly and deliberately) I'm fine, I'm fine.

Larry: Never better, but I think I've had my share.
(Mark picks up another can of beer and begins to talk. Everyone pats him on the back to congratulate him. He responds to everyone's pats by wobbling in the opposite direction)

Narrator: Another hour passed.
(Mark leans on other people and dozes off and on while the others talk)

Mark: Kevin, are you about ready to go home? I'll walk with you.

Kevin: Sure, Mark. Let me get my jacket. (As Kevin goes upstairs to get his jacket, Mark stumbles up the stairs. Kevin returns to the basement with his jacket) Kerrie, have you seen Mark?

Kerrie: He followed you up the stairs, Kevin. I thought you two had left already.

Kevin: He must have gone on home. Are you about ready to go?

Kerrie: Just let me finish this drink.

Kevin: (Sitting down) Sure, I can wait.

Narrator: Outside about a block away, Officer Phillips discovered Mark lying flat in the street. After a quick check, he summoned an ambulance and waited for the paramedics to arrive.
  Two days later, the friends met again at Mark's funeral. After listening to the minister's message, urging them to see Mark's death as a lesson, Kevin responded,

Kevin: I know Mark wouldn't want me to stop having a good time. He'd want me to go on as I have been. But I'll never get smashed like Mark was. I'll be more careful.

What I Learned From Another's Experience

This skit depicts an actual situation of kids trying to have a good time with alcohol.

Check the answers that you think apply and discuss:

To drink that much, Mark must have been . . .

_____ depressed.
_____ trying to prove himself.

_____ celebrating.
_____ enjoying the taste of liquor.

Mark's party friends should have . . .

_____ taken the liquor away from him.
_____ not allowed him to come to the party.
_____ talked him out of drinking so much.

_____ not allowed him to leave the party alone.
_____ done nothing. There's nothing anyone could have done.

The "lesson" in Mark's death is . . .

_____ don't party.
_____ reconsider what you call a "good time."
_____ drinking too much leads to death.

_____ "watch out"—it could happen to you.
(other:) _____
_____

Shade in the beer cans to represent your feelings. For example, if you think drinking's absolutely wrong—shade nothing. If it's absolutely okay—shade the entire can. If you are "in between," shade it accordingly.

Drinking is . . .

   absolutely okay

   absolutely wrong

Parties are . . .

   absolutely okay

   absolutely wrong

For people I know, drinking is . . .

   a great problem

   no problem

If a friend of mine died drinking, I'd . . .

   drink all the more

   never touch a drop

What did I learn?

● How can you help your friends who have a problem with alcohol?
● What can you say and do when a friend is drinking too much at a party?
● Is beer less dangerous than other forms of alcohol? Explain.
● What's the purpose of a party?
● How would you know when a party's "out of hand"?
● What should be done when a party gets out of control?

What Does the Bible Say?

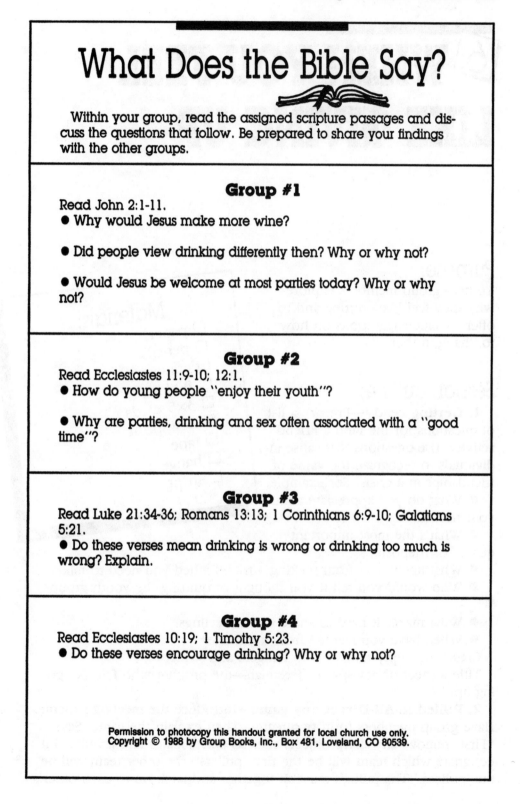

Within your group, read the assigned scripture passages and discuss the questions that follow. Be prepared to share your findings with the other groups.

Group #1

Read John 2:1-11.
● Why would Jesus make more wine?

● Did people view drinking differently then? Why or why not?

● Would Jesus be welcome at most parties today? Why or why not?

Group #2

Read Ecclesiastes 11:9-10; 12:1.
● How do young people "enjoy their youth"?

● Why are parties, drinking and sex often associated with a "good time"?

Group #3

Read Luke 21:34-36; Romans 13:13; 1 Corinthians 6:9-10; Galatians 5:21.
● Do these verses mean drinking is wrong or drinking too much is wrong? Explain.

Group #4

Read Ecclesiastes 10:19; 1 Timothy 5:23.
● Do these verses encourage drinking? Why or why not?

6. WHEN YOU FEEL LIKE GIVING UP

Purpose:

To help group members explore why they feel like quitting and to offer specific suggestions on how to "hang in there."

Session outline:

1. Getting ready—Prepare a list of questions for the Find a Friend activity. Use questions that cause individuals to recognize the value of friendships in a crisis. For example:

● What do you appreciate about your friends?

● What's the most important quality of friendship?

● What keeps you from seeking a friend when you need to talk?

● Who would you tell if you thought of quitting the youth group? Why?

● What makes it hard to share honest feelings?

● When have you learned from a mistake?

Create an empty mobile with hangers and string.

Title a sheet of newsprint "Jeremiah—the prophet who felt like giving up."

2. Pulled-in-All-Directions game—Introduce the meeting's theme. Have group members form two teams. Then explain the game. Say: "First, remove any sharp objects such as belt buckles and jewelry. I'll designate which team will be the first 'pullers'; the other team will be the 'pullees.' The pullees must sit together and latch on to each other's

Materials:
□ paper
□ pencils
□ crayons
□ Bibles
□ 3×5 cards
□ newsprint
□ tape
□ hangers
□ string

arms and legs and hold together as much as possible. The pullers must try to tug the pullees apart. No yanking or rough tugs are allowed. When a pullee gets pulled away from the group, he or she becomes a puller. The object is for all the pullees to be pulled apart."

Play the game, then switch roles. After the game is finished, ask:

● How did you feel during the game?

● What frustrated you?

● Did you ever feel like giving up? Why or why not?

● How would you compare this game to feelings of wanting to quit?

3. I wanted to quit—Give each person paper and crayons. Have members each think of a time when they felt like giving up and draw those feelings. Encourage kids to share their drawings and explain them to the group.

4. Like Jeremiah—Tape the sheet of newsprint on the wall. Have volunteers read the following verses to the group: Jeremiah 1:6; 8:18-22; 14:17-18; 15:18; 20:7-9; 38:5-6; Lamentations 3:7-9, 19-24. After each passage, identify Jeremiah's feelings and list them on the newsprint. Ask: "What did you learn about Jeremiah? about God? How does this apply to your own life?"

5. Find a Friend—Give each person a 3×5 card and a pencil. Say: "We're going to mingle around the room and greet each other. When I shout 'Find a friend,' quickly pair up. I'll ask a question and each of you will have 30 seconds to jot down your partner's answer. I'll call time after 30 seconds to tell you when the other partner should begin. Whenever I say 'Find a friend,' switch partners. Ready? Mingle." Shout: "Find a friend" and ask one of the questions you prepared ahead of time. After 30 seconds, call time and ask the question again. Shout "Find a friend" and continue the activity.

After sufficient time, divide young people into groups no larger than six. Have kids discuss what they learned from this experience.

After the kids' discussions, say: "Sometimes you become discouraged, tired or apathetic with a group even though it once had great meaning and importance in your life. When this happens, you feel like suddenly giving up or gradually becoming inactive. The group doesn't always notice or seem to care. Experts agree that if you drop out and don't become active again within six weeks, it's unlikely you will ever return to the group.

"What can you do when you feel like giving up on a group?

"First, find a friend, someone who is objective and supportive, someone who listens and helps you work through problems rather than hands you pat answers.

"Next, talk about your feelings. Getting rid of negative, hostile feelings is good therapy. Bring them out in the open no matter how cruddy they are.

"Third, learn from your mistakes. Direct your feelings toward a specific issue. Talk about how you feel. Examine the facts and plan how you will avoid the same situation in the future.

"Finally, give it time. Don't give up too quickly on your group. Stay at least three weeks. The group may change, you may change or your feelings may change. Work together to make a conscious effort to change and grow. Anger and hurts heal faster within a group of individuals who are important to you, so 'hang in there.' "

6. Hang in there—Have each group member write on a 3×5 card a word of hope and encouragement to remember when a person feels like giving up. Give each person a piece of tape. Gather group members in a circle around the empty mobile. Close with a "hang in there" prayer: Have each person, one at a time, repeat his or her word of hope and tape the card to the mobile. Close with a group hug.

Keep the mobile hanging for a while as a reminder of the group's support.

7. JOB STRESS

Purpose:
To meet the needs of group members who have jobs or plan to have jobs in the future.

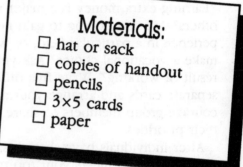

Materials:
- ☐ hat or sack
- ☐ copies of handout
- ☐ pencils
- ☐ 3×5 cards
- ☐ paper

Session outline:

1. Getting ready—Select an appropriate meeting time that accommodates as many working kids as possible. Consider doing the meeting more than once if necessary—to let working kids know you care.

Have an artistic young person design and make copies of an imaginary "paycheck" for the closing prayer time. Encourage the artist to have fun with the design and make it look like a large check. Leave space for group members to fill in their prayer concerns for the recipient instead of entering a cash value. Provide space for the youth group's name or for all group members to sign.

Copy each of the following "Work Attitude Statements" on a 3×5 card. Pass them out to different individuals and ask them to read these statements in order when you give them the signal.

- I can't take it anymore. I never get to do anything *I* want to do.
- Everyone at work thinks I'm lazy.
- All the customers yell at me.
- I never have time to be with friends because I'm always busy.
- I'm flunking math and Spanish.
- I'm missing all the fun things at church and school.
- I'm exhausted.

2. Work attitudes—Have the group sit in a circle. Ask each member to portray silently how he or she feels about working. Remember: No words! For example, someone might pretend to count dollar bills, another might fall backward in exhaustion. Talk about what each person did. Ask: "What kinds of stress did you see? What other forms of job stress have you experienced (your own or someone else's)?"

Signal the kids with the cards to read their statements in order.

Say: "Do these statements sound familiar? You can probably understand these kinds of job-related pressures, especially since many of you or your friends work.

"With school, relationships, church and extracurricular involvements, a job usually multiplies the stress you feel. So, how can you deal with the pressures brought on by holding a job? This meeting will give you tips to help make the responsibilities of a job more manageable and enjoyable."

3. Expectation evaluation—Give each person five 3×5 cards. Say: "Earning extra money is a major reason for working, but what about others? Are you hoping to gain new skills, make new friends, get experience in a particular field, or work in an area that might help you make a vocational choice? Ask yourself, 'What do I hope to gain as a result of working?' Write five different answers to this question on separate cards and arrange your answers in order of importance." Encourage group members to share their answers and the reasons for their priorities.

After individuals have shared, say: "If you're looking for a job, try to find one that meets your top three priorities. If you work now, evaluate your current job in light of what you hope to gain from being employed. If your current job doesn't fit your priorities, explain those priorities to your supervisor and negotiate alternatives. If there are no alternatives, try to get another job. When your job doesn't meet your expectations, you will always feel stressed."

4. Fresh perspectives—Tell the group: "Another way to approach stress on the job is to broaden your perspective. Look for new ways to view what you do!"

One by one, have each person sit in the center of the circle and describe his or her job. Next have all the other members give as many creative "fresh perspectives" concerning that job as they can. For example, if Patty takes orders at a fast-food restaurant, members could say she helps by feeding people, brightening their day, smiling, being a positive person or saving time for busy people.

5. The extra mile—Say: "When you see how your job benefits others, it makes it easier to do things people don't expect. Offer a helping hand, give someone a smile, compliment work well-done. This positive attitude makes a job more enjoyable for you and for those for whom and with whom you work."

Have each teenager write on a slip of paper a tough situation he or she has encountered at work, a time when it was hard to go the extra mile. Place all the slips of paper in a hat or sack. Have kids draw one situation at a time, role play it, and offer "extra mile" suggestions. Have fun with it; spark new ways working kids can reflect their Christian faith.

6. Spiritual support—Pass out the "How Does God Fit in With My Job?" handout. Allow a few minutes for individuals to complete the questions. Ask them to share at least two responses with the rest of the group.

Say: "It's easy to neglect your spiritual life when you think your time is already overscheduled. It helps to stay active in church and the youth group. No matter how much you need money, don't let your job separate you from Christian fellowship and worship.

"Also, remember the importance of spending personal time with God each day. You may have to make time by getting up early. But make nurturing your relationship with Christ the first order of each day.

"Think about why you are working. If you're working only to earn money to spend on yourself, check your priorities. On the other hand, your job can also give you opportunities to share God's love. Earning money can give you a chance to pass on a portion of your earnings to the church or some missionary outreach you feel strongly about. Also, if you are honest, work hard and relate personably to staff and customers, you'll present an example some of your co-workers may have never seen. Your actions on the job will share your faith in a visible way!"

7. "Paycheck" prayers—Give each person a paycheck with his or her name on it. Pass all the checks around the circle and use them for members to offer written, one-word prayer concerns. Ask each person to fill in a prayer concern for the recipient of the check. For example, (pay them) patience, support, guidance.

As the checks are moving around the room, remind the group to take time for play. Say: "Research shows that all work and no play can make you unhappy. Waking early for school, going directly to work after classes and returning home late at night to crash into bed is simply not the way to live. When Jesus spoke of the abundant life, he meant that you can experience a re-creation through recreation. Remember to make time for 'playing.'

"Talk with your parents about the pressures. Your parents want you to learn about responsibility, but not at the expense of unreasonable physical, emotional or spiritual stress. Talk with them. Learn from their wisdom and years of experience. Let them be a source of support and comfort. They may have ideas about how to get your work done more easily, quickly and enjoyably.

"Christ wants each person to experience the fullness of life and this experience includes your job. Psalm 20:4 reads, 'May he give you the desire of your heart and make all your plans succeed.' ''

When everyone's completed paycheck returns to the recipient, have each person read aloud his or her paycheck as a prayer.

KEEP GOING!

How Does God Fit in With My Job ??

Complete the following sentences and share at least two of these with the group.

1. Since I started work, my spiritual life has _____

_____ .

2. I know God is with me in my work because _____

_____ .

3. It's hard to stay involved in church because _____

_____ .

4. My personal time with God is _____

_____ .

5. I use the money I make for _____

_____ .

6. On the job, I feel God's presence when _____

_____ .

7. I feel my parents' concern about me and my job when _____

_____ .

8. When I feel stress or pressure on the job, I _____

_____ .

9. My best support on my job is _____

_____ .

8. SURVIVING THE TOUGH STUFF

Purpose:
To help group members develop a positive attitude toward personal hardship.

Materials:
- ☐ several blindfolds
- ☐ tape
- ☐ get-well cards
- ☐ orange juice
- ☐ crackers
- ☐ copies of handouts
- ☐ Bibles
- ☐ pencils

Session outline:

1. Put yourself in their shoes—Divide the group into three or more groups for "simulated handicap" experiences. Blindfold members of the first group. Tape each member's thumbs to his or her hands in the second group. Have members of the third group each keep one hand behind their back. Then have kids untie and tie a shoelace—their own or someone else's if their shoes don't have laces. Ask: "How did you feel about not being able to function as you usually do? How would you survive if you had no eyes, two deformed hands or only one hand? How would you feel?"

2. First-person account—Invite a Christian teenager or adult with a handicap (for example, blindness, injured or missing limb, paralysis) to attend the meeting. Ask your guest to briefly tell how God has helped him or her survive the handicap. Allow time for group members to question your guest about the impact of the handicap on his or her daily life, faith in God, Christian witness, etc.

3. "Diagnose Your Illness"—Divide the group into pairs. Give each group member a copy of the "Diagnose Your Illness" handout. Have pairs diagnose the "handicaps" (tough situations) they or their friends are facing at school, home or work. Encourage pairs to share their diagnoses with the whole group.

4. Write prescriptions—Move pairs into groups of four or six. Give each person a copy of the "RX" handout and assign each group one of the three scripture passages at the top. Have groups complete the prescription exercise as directed on the handout. Then have each group share its prescription with the whole group by presenting a two-minute skit in the office of Dr. U.R. Surviving.

5. Get-well cards—Pass out get-well cards. Have kids write notes of encouragement on the cards to give to someone facing a difficult situation.

6. Hospital food—Serve orange juice and crackers.

THERE'S MORE!

Diagnose Your Illness

Imagine that Dr. U.R. Surviving, the famous specialist in teenage handicaps, has moved his practice to your town. He wants to help you and your friends, but he needs information from you. How would you answer his interview questions?

1. What are the "handicaps" (tough situations) you and your friends are facing at school? at home? at work?

2. Do some of these situations make you "sicker" than others? Explain.

3. What causes these handicaps?

4. What can you do to overcome them?

RX

Read your assigned verses and write a prescription for overcoming difficulties based on your findings. Be prepared to act out your prescription in a two-minute skit in the office of Dr. U.R. Surviving.

1. Proverbs 30:5; Jeremiah 29:11; Luke 5:31.

2. Romans 8:28, 35-39.

3. 2 Corinthians 4:16-18; 12:7-10.

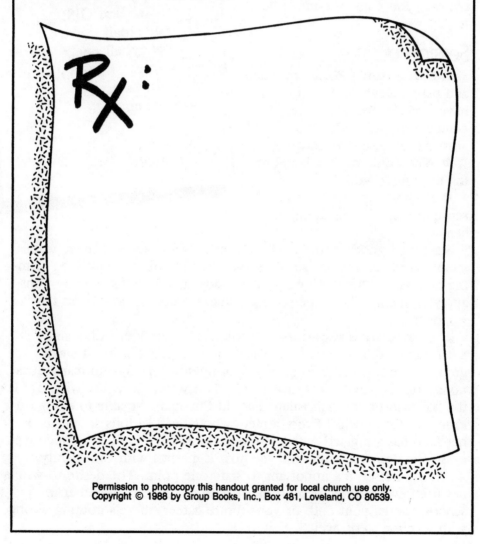

R:

9. WANTING TO WIN

Purpose:
To help group members explore the pros and cons of competition.

Session outline:

1. Game time—Form two teams and play volleyball. After the teams have experienced some healthy competition, have kids write their answers to these questions:

- When did you feel best during the game? worst?
- How would you describe the sense of competition during the game?

Materials:
- [ ] volleyball
- [ ] volleyball net
- [ ] copies of handouts
- [ ] name tags
- [ ] markers
- [ ] Bibles
- [ ] paper
- [ ] pencils

Next, play another round of volleyball. Only this time, have team members trade sides after each serve. Players will constantly be forming new teams. After the game, have kids answer the same questions, applying them only to the second game. Compare and discuss their responses.

2. Competitive thoughts—Distribute the handout "Choosing Sides" and explain the directions to the group. When most small groups have finished talking, say: "Competition brings up many questions, and they aren't easy to answer. Is it wrong to enjoy winning? Is the 'killer instinct' unchristian? Should Christians be able to shrug off losing as 'God's will'? Every athlete who's been serious about his or her faith has struggled with these questions. Let's look at competitiveness—the desire to win—and see how it meshes with Christianity.

"At the outset, it's important to state one point: The desire to win is not itself evil; neither is any other desire to succeed. Whether in school, sports, your faith or your future career, there's nothing wrong with wanting to do well.

"Christians can have a hard time accepting this. After all, aren't we supposed to give up everything for Christ? If we want something, doesn't that automatically mean it's bad? But the Bible doesn't teach that simply wanting something is wrong.

"On the other hand, success isn't automatically right, either. To contradict the great coach Vince Lombardi, winning *isn't* everything. When winning becomes a god, sports are harmful. Let's take a balanced look at competitiveness—the good and the bad. That way you can compete, enjoy it and grow from it."

3. Good and bad lessons—Divide group members into three groups by spelling the word WIN. Then divide each group in half to form six groups. Pass out the "Competitiveness: Good or Bad?" handout and assign a lesson to each small group. After a few minutes, ask the groups to share their findings.

4. "Attitude Scoreboard"—Distribute the handout and encourage people to discuss their answers within the small groups.

5. "What Does the Bible Say?"—Pass out the handout and ask the groups to discuss all three questions.

When most groups have finished, say: "On the one hand, no one is commanding you to hang up your uniform and enjoy less 'worldly' pursuits. But on the other hand, be aware of your thoughts and feelings. Can you compete without hating your opponent? Is your self-image tied to the outcome, so much that losing destroys you? Do sports come between you and God? You see, Christianity and sports can mix, but Christianity has to come first. If you find you simply can't compete and reflect your Christian character, it might be wise to take time off to get your head and heart together.

"This kind of drastic action is rarely necessary. Chances are, you can enjoy sports and please God at the same time. Just 'go out there and give it all you've got' in both areas, and you'll come out a winner."

6. Athletes' feet—Have kids each place one of their shoes in the center of the group. Have them make a name tag for their shoe so people know whose it is. Provide slips of paper and pencils so group members can write "winning" comments—encouragement and support for one another. Tell them to put a positive-statement slip in each person's shoe for him or her to read later.

7. Running the race—Form teams of four by grouping four different shoes together. Give each team a Bible and instructions to read Philippians 3:12-14. Assign each team a sport such as football, tennis, gymnastics or baseball. Have the groups paraphrase the scripture, using their assigned sport.

Close by having teams share their "sport" scripture with the large group.

8. For small groups—To build a spirit of competitiveness, play Newspaper Flurry. Form two teams—as small as one person per team. Have the teams face each other. Stretch a rope or string across the room between the teams by tying it to two chairs. Provide a stack of newspapers for each team. The object: Teams wad up and toss the newspapers across the rope so the least amount of paper ends up on their side of the rope. Allow about three minutes for the flurry.

After the flurry, have kids describe their feelings about the game—the fury or fun of competition. You could also discuss how they feel about being a small group; if they feel competitive sizewise with other youth groups; and what competitiveness does to youth groups.

Create only three groups with the word WIN. Give each group both a good and a bad lesson to read about and share with the other groups.

Choosing Sides

What are your thoughts concerning Christianity and sports? Check your response to each thought and situation below. Discuss your answers with one or two people sitting next to you.

1. The desire to win is not itself evil.

Agree_____   Disagree_____

2. Winning isn't everything; it's the only thing.

Agree_____   Disagree_____

3. Dealing with sports-related disappointments now will help you later in life.

Agree_____   Disagree_____

4. Losing to a fine player is more rewarding than beating a beginner.

Agree_____   Disagree_____

5. You can enjoy sports and please God at the same time.

Agree_____   Disagree_____

6. You're playing your best friend in a lively game of tennis. It's a tough match; you've split the first two sets. You desperately want to win the third set. Is that . . .

Right_____   Wrong_____

7. Your high school football team's opponent boasts the top receiver in the county, and you're assigned to cover him. He's been beating you all night. You decide you're going to try to injure him and put him out of the game. After all, he's keeping your team from winning, and you want to help your team. Is that . . .

Right_____   Wrong_____

8. Your high school basketball team is playing the best team in the league. The teams battle through two overtimes, but the other team pulls it out on a last-second basket. After the game, you're depressed. Is that . . .

Right_____   Wrong_____

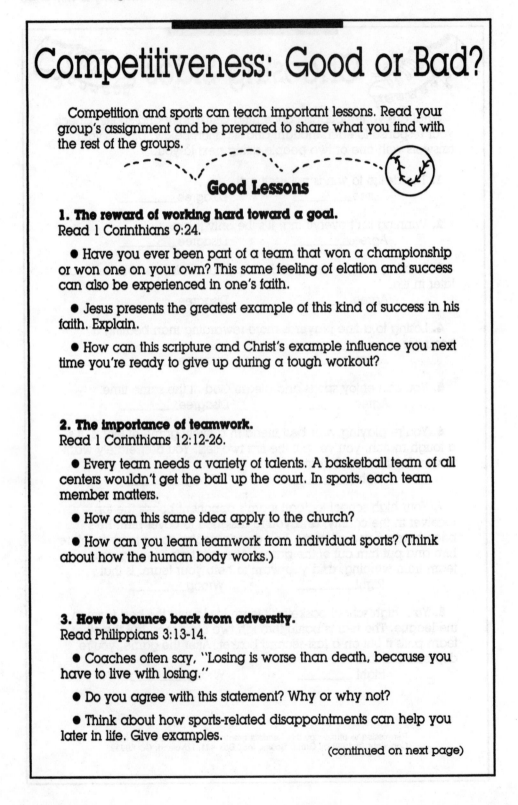

Competitiveness: Good or Bad?

Competition and sports can teach important lessons. Read your group's assignment and be prepared to share what you find with the rest of the groups.

Good Lessons

1. The reward of working hard toward a goal.
Read 1 Corinthians 9:24.

● Have you ever been part of a team that won a championship or won one on your own? This same feeling of elation and success can also be experienced in one's faith.

● Jesus presents the greatest example of this kind of success in his faith. Explain.

● How can this scripture and Christ's example influence you next time you're ready to give up during a tough workout?

2. The importance of teamwork.
Read 1 Corinthians 12:12-26.

● Every team needs a variety of talents. A basketball team of all centers wouldn't get the ball up the court. In sports, each team member matters.

● How can this same idea apply to the church?

● How can you learn teamwork from individual sports? (Think about how the human body works.)

3. How to bounce back from adversity.
Read Philippians 3:13-14.

● Coaches often say, "Losing is worse than death, because you have to live with losing."

● Do you agree with this statement? Why or why not?

● Think about how sports-related disappointments can help you later in life. Give examples.

(continued on next page)

Bad Lessons

1. Hating your opponent.
Read Luke 6:27-28.

One misconception in sports is that you have to hate your opponent or else you can't win. But this isn't true. Your main competition isn't your opponent; it's you. What does this statement mean?

Would God want you to participate in sports if you'd have to hate people?

Next time you're in an athletic contest, don't look at your opponent as someone who's keeping you from reaching a goal or trying to take something you want (victory). Look at him or her as someone who's giving you the opportunity to do your best, and as someone you can help do the same.

2. Associating personal worth with winning and losing.
Read Ephesians 2:8-10.

There's nothing wrong with feeling bad about losing. But it's easy to take that too far and tie your self-image to the scoreboard. After all, there's so much pressure—from coaches, schoolmates and even parents—that it's easy to feel worthless when you lose.

Why do you feel worthless when you lose?

If winning is so important, you can always find people to beat. You could find plenty of beginners to drag onto the tennis court and whip. But that's not the reason to compete.

What is the reason to compete?

3. Losing perspective.
Read 1 Corinthians 10:31.

Too often, winning becomes the god. Respond to the following statements:

Leo Durocher, a Hall of Fame baseball pitcher: "If it's under W for Win, nobody asks you how."

Bob Goldman, author of *Death in the Locker Room*: "I asked 198 top world-class athletes . . . 'If I had a magic drug that was so fantastic that if you took it once you would win every competition you would enter . . . (but) it would kill you five years after you took it, would you still take the drug?' Fifty-two percent said yes."

Attitude Scoreboard

How about your competitive mind-set? For each sports-related situation, circle the number that best represents your answer. Discuss your answers within your small group.

1. All through a game, your opponent taunts and insults you. Your opponent's team wins. What do you do after the game?

1	2	3	4	5	6	7	8	9	10

Smile, shake hands and congratulate him or her

Shake hands without smiling

Ignore him or her

2. You've surprised everyone by making the finals of the conference tennis tournament. You play the top seed and lose, 7-6, 7-5. How do you feel?

1	2	3	4	5	6	7	8	9	10

Disappointed, but pleased that you played so well and made it as far as you did

A little sad that you made it so far, only to lose

Angry at yourself for blowing key points and losing a match you should have won

3. You have a chance to play on a county all-star soccer team. One catch: Practices are held on Sunday mornings. What do you do?

1	2	3	4	5	6	7	8	9	10

Turn it down and trust another opportunity will come along

Try to strike a deal with the coach to make half the practices

Join the all-star team

What Does the Bible Say?

Read the following Bible passages and answer the questions. Discuss your answers within your group.

1. "And Jesus grew in wisdom and stature, and in favor with God and men" (Luke 2:52).
Do you think Jesus participated in sports as a child? as a teenager? as a young man? Why or why not?

2. "If anyone competes as an athlete, he does not receive the victor's crown unless he competes according to the rules" (2 Timothy 2:5).
How would you feel about a Christian athlete who takes steroids because they make him or her a better athlete? who intentionally breaks the rules because it helps him or her win?

3. "I have fought the good fight, I have finished the race, I have kept the faith. Now there is in store for me the crown of righteousness" (2 Timothy 4:7-8).
In what ways does athletic discipline help you as a Christian?

10. HOW TO SURVIVE YOUR YOUTH LEADER'S HIGH EXPECTATIONS

Purpose:

To help group members set realistic goals for their involvement in the church's youth ministry.

Session outline:

1. Build a "card house"— Have group members form groups of three. Give each small group a deck of playing cards with the instructions to build the biggest

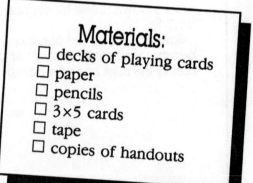

Materials:
- ☐ decks of playing cards
- ☐ paper
- ☐ pencils
- ☐ 3×5 cards
- ☐ tape
- ☐ copies of handouts

"card house" they can. Allow five minutes for the activity. (It's not easy and takes a lot of cooperation.) Use the activity to lead into dealing with high expectations.

Bring the group together and have each person respond to the open-ended statement, "A time I felt pressured by high expectations was when . . ."

2. "I Feel Taken for Granted"—Next have one young person read the monologue, "I Feel Taken for Granted." Ask:
- Is this problem similar to your own situation? Why or why not?
- What advice would you give this person?
- Who is responsible for the person feeling this way? Why?

Say: "Does all this pressure sound familiar? Dealing with another adult's high expectations can be as pressure-filled as coping with your parents' demands for better and better grades. Most of you *want* to be involved in youth group activities. Your involvement makes you feel valuable. Helping with preparations and assuming leadership responsibilities offer a way to feel good about yourself. From early childhood all of you have learned that doing things for others, and doing them right, brings positive results. But problems balloon when you don't recognize your limits.

"Look around you. High achievers are everywhere—dreaming big dreams and setting high goals, sometimes unrealistic goals. Those unrealistic goals often link with others' high expectations: 'Yes, I'll make those calls for you.' 'Yes, I'll volunteer to plan and organize another youth retreat.' 'Yes . . . yes . . . yes . . .' When you run out of energy, your inability to get everything done leads to problems.

"You may become depressed. Deep inside you may think, 'If I don't help, I'm a bad person.' Even though you know that's not true, you mysteriously believe it. And when that foglike anxiety closes in, anger results and you explode, 'I can't humanly do everything everyone expects of me!'

"If you've experienced this kind of depression or irritability, think about the reasons. Get in touch with your actions and attitudes."

3. Learning limits—Say: "There *are* ways to cope. Recognize your limits, learn to say no, and get feedback from other people." Pass out copies of the handout "Be Aware of Your Limits." Go through the directions and have each person work independently on this activity. After 10 minutes, have each person share his or her discoveries with a partner.

4. "Learn to Say No"—Pass out the handout "Learn to Say No." Have group members practice saying no to their partners in each of the situations. Discuss:

● How does it feel to say no to a leader, a parent or a teacher?

● Why is it so difficult to say no to these people?

Share with your young people how you feel when a young person tells you no.

5. Check with others—Form small groups of four or less. Have each person tell who he or she talks with to get helpful advice. Discuss the following questions:

● What do you say or do when an adult you talk with offers an answer or a comment you weren't prepared to hear?

● How can you help each other as group members deal with adults' high expectations?

● What are ways you can help each other not to feel overloaded?

6. Be honest—Bring everyone together and read Ephesians 4:15. Say, "This is an opportunity for each one of us to be honest with one another." Talk for one or two minutes about your time commitments and expectations for the group. Ask the kids to share the same about themselves. Tell them to explain their feelings and let the group know what's going on in their lives. You may discover some are working to pay family bills, while others are getting up at 5 a.m. for gymnastics practice. Some may mention some tension between spending time with their families and spending time at church. Encourage everyone to be up front and honest by exhibiting these qualities yourself.

Talk about how it feels when young people are honest with you. Tell the group: "Don't say you have other commitments if you really don't. If you don't want to do what's been asked, say so! If I ask you to make phone calls and you detest calling people, don't say, 'No, I'm too busy.' Instead say, 'No, I feel uncomfortable making phone calls.' That lessens the frustration for both of us. Honesty lets me know what you *like* to do. All of us have different gifts to offer. God wants us to feel good about giving those gifts!"

Distribute paper and a pencil to each person. Invite everyone to write a note to you about his or her involvement with the youth group. Say: "This is a great opportunity for you to let me know if you are overwhelmed or would like more responsibility. Sign your notes and pass them to me as soon as you are finished."

7. Gift-building—Give each person four 3×5 cards. Encourage kids to think about the different gifts, abilities and talents they can contribute to the church's youth ministry. Have them write one gift, ability or talent on each card.

Say: "It's up to you now. You are responsible for developing the skills necessary to cope with others' high expectations. So when you feel ready to quit, slow down and evaluate the best way you can serve as part of Christ's body."

As a prayer of thanks, have each person share his or her cards and work together to create a "card house" by taping each other's cards together. Keep the structure around for a few weeks as a reminder of what young people can offer the church.

I Feel Taken for Granted

(Monologue)

Read this monologue ahead of time and read it to the group at the beginning of this session.

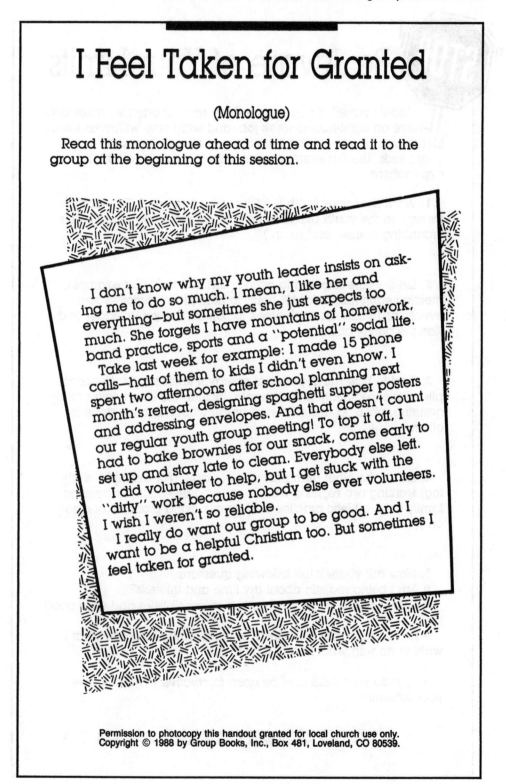

I don't know why my youth leader insists on asking me to do so much. I mean, I like her and everything—but sometimes she just expects too much. She forgets I have mountains of homework, band practice, sports and a "potential" social life.

Take last week for example: I made 15 phone calls—half of them to kids I didn't even know. I spent two afternoons after school planning next month's retreat, designing spaghetti supper posters and addressing envelopes. And that doesn't count our regular youth group meeting! To top it off, I had to bake brownies for our snack, come early to set up and stay late to clean. Everybody else left.

I did volunteer to help, but I get stuck with the "dirty" work because nobody else ever volunteers. I wish I weren't so reliable.

I really do want our group to be good. And I want to be a helpful Christian too. But sometimes I feel taken for granted.

STOP Be Aware of Your Limits

Know yourself. If you require three hours a day for homework, have an eight-hour-a-week job, and want time with your family, friends and church—weigh the time and energy necessary to fulfill your needs. Use this exercise to set limits in dealing with high expectations.

1. What does your youth leader expect from you? (For example, serving on the youth planning committee, providing refreshments, organizing games, and so on.)

2. List the time required to accomplish that task. (For example, meeting each month for 1½ hours to help plan "major" youth events, or 15 minutes each week to contact the youth leader and start the phone chain.)

3. Decide how much personal energy it takes for you to accomplish this expectation. (For example, include the time it takes for organizing, phoning and following up on what has been done by others.)

4. List all the other demands on your time. (For example, studying, working two nights a week, watching television, babysitting, family time, athletic practice and events, band practice, and so on.)

5. Now ask yourself the following questions:
● Am I being realistic about my time and interests?
● Can I say yes to the youth group responsibilities and do a good job?
● Do I need to make a choice or compromise between what I want to do with what I have time to do?

Recognize your limits and be open to creative ways to juggle your schedule.

Learn to Say No

It's hard to say no to others' requests, especially your youth leader's. When you want that special person to like you and accept you, it's difficult to risk his or her anger or disappointment. An adult, however, will appreciate your honesty if you're genuinely overloaded. Saying no is one way to display your responsible behavior and time management skills. After setting realistic limits for yourself, trust that saying no can sometimes be the right answer.

Practice saying no to your partner in each of these situations.

1. You have a term paper due tomorrow. Your youth leader calls to see if you want to go to the movie with her and some other kids from the group.

2. The new youth leader stops you after the meeting to ask if you could head the phone chain committee. He doesn't know that you hate to talk on the phone.

3. Tonight is the last night of the television miniseries you've been watching for the last six weeks. You've been excited about it all week. The youth minister calls and wants to visit with you tonight about this weekend's retreat.

4. The youth group has made plans for a weekend ski trip. Your little brother's ball game was moved to Friday night, so you were planning to meet everyone at the mountain on Saturday morning. The youth leader calls to see if you're still planning to present the evening worship you volunteered for on Friday night when everyone arrives.

5. You are on your way out the door to a youth group committee meeting when the phone rings. Your dad asks you to straighten the house and get supper started since he's bringing his boss home for dinner. No one else is home, and you're chairperson of the committee.

SECTION THREE:

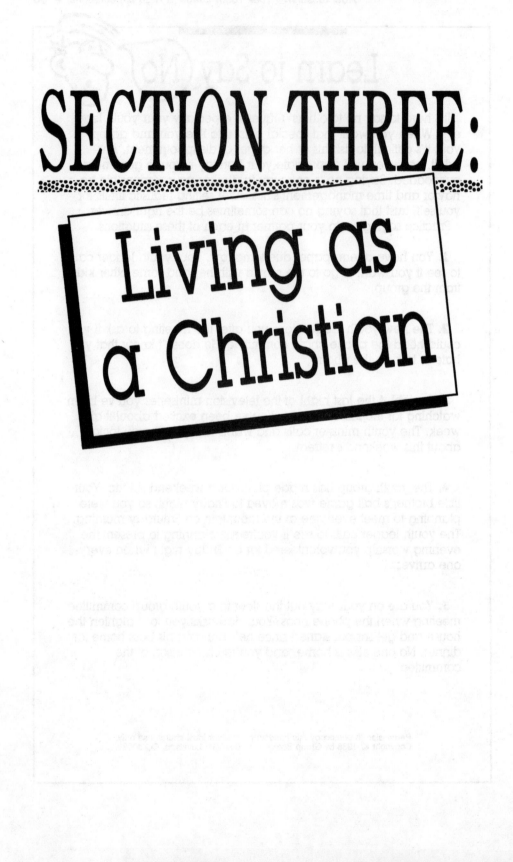

Living as a Christian

11. ARE YOU A SATURDAY NIGHT/ SUNDAY MORNING CHRISTIAN?

Purpose:

To help group members participate in a thought-provoking discussion of hypocrisy.

Session outline:

1. Face value—As kids come in, have them create two-sided paper plate masks: one side angry or unhappy and the other smiling. Explain that the angry/unhappy side is Saturday night, and the other is Sunday morning.

2. Counterfeit Christians—Have the kids pair off with a friend. Say: "Sometimes your Saturday night actions don't reflect your Sunday morning faith. But that doesn't mean you are a counterfeit Christian. You may, however, experience some counterfeit feelings and sometimes feel unworthy to be called Christian. It's okay to recognize that you aren't perfect and that you will sin, and yet go on living a life based on God's principles of love and decency."

Move the group into pairs. Give one member of each pair a copy of "Paul's Advice to the Counterfeit Christian" and the other member a copy of "King David's Advice to the Counterfeit Christian." Have in-

Materials:
- ☐ paper plates
- ☐ colored markers
- ☐ newsprint
- ☐ copies of handouts
- ☐ Bibles
- ☐ pencils

dividuals write their responses and share them with their partners.

3. Hypocrisy scale—Divide kids into three groups. Have individuals complete "A Sinner's Hypocrisy Scale" and discuss it in their groups.

4. About faces—Tell each group to read one of these Bible accounts: Luke 15:1-32; John 8:1-11; Acts 5:1-11. Have the individual groups act out their passages before the large group, wearing their masks. The group members turn their paper plate masks in whichever direction best reflects their character's attitude. When appropriate, the characters turn their masks around.

5. Talking it over—Gather the groups back together. Discuss the main characters from each Bible story. Ask: "Were characters mainly 'Saturday Night' or 'Sunday Morning' Christians? Explain. What can we learn from each of them?" Write responses on newsprint.

6. Closing—Gather the group into a circle. Put the newsprint in the center and have kids place their masks on the floor, happy face up. Then join hands. Pray that group members grow in their acceptance of themselves and their ability to be consistent Christians.

Paul's Advice to the Counterfeit Christian

Below is a letter written to the apostle Paul from a teenager who is feeling like a counterfeit Christian. Read the letter and the scripture passage. Then write a letter of advice as Paul might have written it.

Dear Paul:

Last night I blew it. I went to this party and things really got out of hand. The problem is, this isn't the first time. I'm supposed to be a Christian, but I'm always doing things I know I shouldn't do. I can't tell anyone about it. Everyone knows I'm a Christian. I can't even pray. Maybe I'm not a Christian after all. Christians don't do those things. I guess I'm just a phony. What should I do?

Feeling Phony

Read Romans 7:15-25. Answer this letter the way you think Paul would have answered it.

DEAR FEELING PHONY:

GRACE AND PEACE,
PAUL

King David's Advice to the Counterfeit Christian

Below is a letter written to King David from a teenager who is feeling like a counterfeit Christian. Read the letter and the scripture passage. Then write a letter of advice as David might have written it.

Dear King David:

It is getting harder and harder for me to go to church. I sit there and listen to our pastor talk about the things Christians should be doing. I don't do many of those things. I don't go out and witness. I don't read my Bible much either. I guess maybe I'm not a Christian after all. Maybe I should just bag church. What do you think I should do?

Down and Almost Out

Read Psalm 51:10-13 and Psalm 5:7. Answer this letter the way you think King David would have answered it.

Dear Down and Almost Out:

Blessed be the Lord,
King David

A Sinner's Hypocrisy Scale

Asking whether you're really a Christian is a bit like asking how you can tell whether you really love your mother. It's not a simple matter of keeping track of things you do, how often you speak to God or how often you displease him.

The following questions will help you think about the sincerity of your faith. For each statement, mark an "X" on the spot on the continuum that best represents your answer.

Think carefully about the meaning of your answers.

1. I am in touch with God other than at special times such as worship.

_____ never

_____
always

2. I measure my faith by comparing myself to other people.

_____ never

_____
always

3. I think of faith as "fire insurance" to use "just in case."

_____ never

_____
always

4. I recognize myself as a human being who can never fully please God.

_____ never

_____
always

5. In spite of repeated failures, I sincerely want to live a God-pleasing life.

_____ never

_____
always

6. I'm confident Christ lived and died so I can be free from sin.

_____ never

_____
always

12. IS GOING TO CHURCH REALLY NECESSARY?

Purpose:
To help group members evaluate the importance of church for themselves.

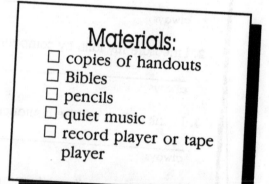

Materials:
- ☐ copies of handouts
- ☐ Bibles
- ☐ pencils
- ☐ quiet music
- ☐ record player or tape player

Session outline:

1. "Search Me"—Pass out Bibles, pencils and the "Search Me" handout. After 15 minutes, ask young people to divide into groups of three to six and discuss their answers.

2. Excuses, excuses—Say: "Lots of people wonder whether going to church is a 'have to.' So they make choices. The trouble is, many people choose to avoid church because they've come up with some convincing excuses like: 'I worship God in my own way.' 'I used to go—but I don't need to anymore.' 'I see God in nature.' 'I watch a preacher on television.'

"What were some of the excuses you heard when you were discussing the 'Search Me' handout? What other excuses have you heard?

"All excuses aside, does a person really have to go to church to be a Christian?"

3. "God's Idea"—Say: "Going to church shouldn't be a 'have to' set of meaningless motions. It needs to be a time for cultivating a relationship with the one who loves you more than anyone else. God doesn't need us to go to church to prove anything. We are the ones who need church. We need time to work at this relationship.

"Let's look at three of God's reasons we should go to church."

Divide young people into three groups. Pass out the "God's Idea" handout, and assign one boldface statement to each group. Ask groups to read the suggested scripture passages and list ways the church can be this kind of place. Ask groups to share their lists with the other groups. After each group shares, say: "All three statements offer us an opportunity to examine ourselves more closely in God's eyes. Think about the questions 'How do I need to connect, reflect and respond?' Write your answers in the blanks underneath each question. Share your answers with the rest of the people in your small group."

4. Your decision—Ask group members to lay down in a circle with their heads facing the center. Have them close their eyes and relax. Dim the lights and play some quiet music for a few minutes. After everyone has relaxed, say: "It's Sunday morning. You've scrunched the pillow around your head to muffle your alarm clock's annoying clatter. You're not sure you want to go to church today, so you start making excuses. 'Church is boring.' 'Nobody cares if I'm there or not.' 'All they want is my money.' 'Everybody is a hypocrite.' 'My faith is just between God and me.' Lay there a few moments and decide what you're going to do."

After about one minute, ask the group members to open their eyes, stretch and sit up. Close by saying: "Let's face it, there are numerous reasons for not going to church. The church will never be perfect. Sermons will be boring, people will speak unkind words, and the church leaders will make mistakes.

"But don't give up. People make the church imperfect, but God can make it perfect. Accept the shortcomings and failures of the people in your church—yourself included! Focus on God's incredible love in action.

"Think about the choice you made earlier. Pray silently for God's guidance and support as you continue to make that choice each week.

"Ask the person on your right to pray for you too. With God's support and the support of a friend, you will recognize the church in action."

KEEP GOING

Search Me

Choose the best answers for you. Then discuss why you made those choices with the rest of your small group.

1. For me, going to church is most like . . .

2. When someone says "church," I immediately think of . . .
- a person. ☐
- a place. ☐
- an activity. ☐
- other: _____

4. So you don't feel like going to church? What's your reason?
- I have to work. ☐
- I'm just plain lazy. ☐
- Church is boring. ☐
- I stayed out too late the night before. ☐
- My parents don't go, so why should I? ☐
- other: _____

3. Right now for me, church is a . . .
- "have to." ☐
- "want to." ☐
- "need to." ☐

5. List by name four different types of people who go to your church. (For example, a grandparent, new baby, college student and so on.) Then list two unique characteristics each person contributes to the "body."

NAME
Example: Grandma Kraft

QUALITIES
Example: Wisdom and giving of time

1. _____   _____
2. _____   _____
3. _____   _____
4. _____   _____
(You)_____   (Your qualities)_____

What surprised you about the people listed? Did some characteristics overlap? Why or why not? What does this tell you about being joined with different people? How does that make the church unique and exciting?

6. See what the following verses say about the church:
1 Corinthians 12:4-27   Romans 12:4-8
Ephesians 2:19-22   1 Peter 2:5-9

(continued on next page)

7. Checkmark (✔) six words that describe how you've felt about yourself this past week:

angry	all-together	uncomfortable	unimportant
pleased	all-alone	comfortable	empty
worthless	strong	loved	full
valuable	weak	unloved	content
giving	glad	real	discontent
selfish	sad	fake	forgiven
great	good	important	unforgiven
small	bad		

Now star (★) six words you'd use to describe God this past week.
Did any words overlap? Why or why not? Could they? Should they?
Explain.

Now circle six words that describe what you'd *like* to feel about yourself. Were they different from the first set of checkmarked words? Why or why not?

8. List five talents/gifts/abilities/resources you can give to your church. Write how and when you plan to use them.

	Offering	How I'll give it	When
1.	_____	_____	_____
2.	_____	_____	_____
3.	_____	_____	_____
4.	_____	_____	_____
5.	_____	_____	_____

9. What I really like about my church is . . .

10. My church would be "perfect" if . . .

11. What would you say?

Do you have to go to church to be a Christian?

God's Idea

Read the scripture for your assigned statement and list ways the church can be this kind of place. After listening to each group's report, decide how the church can provide a place for you to connect, reflect and respond.

1. Church is a place to connect.
(1 Corinthians 12:4-27)

_____
_____
_____
_____

How do I need to *connect*?

_____
_____
_____

2. Church is a place to *reflect*.
(Psalm 46:10)

_____
_____
_____

How do I need to *reflect*?

_____
_____
_____

3. Church is a place to *respond*.
(Acts 20:35)

_____
_____
_____
_____
_____

How do I need to *respond*?

_____
_____
_____
_____
_____

13. TURNING PEOPLE OFF TO CHRISTIANITY

Purpose:
To help group members effectively tell about and show others their faith in God.

Session outline:

1. Vacuum-cleaner price—Set a vacuum cleaner in the middle of the room. As kids come in, ask them to write on 3×5 cards what they think the vacuum cleaner costs. The person guessing closest to the actual price wins a whisk broom.

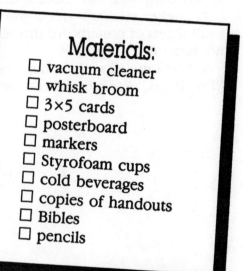

Materials:
- [ ] vacuum cleaner
- [ ] whisk broom
- [ ] 3×5 cards
- [ ] posterboard
- [ ] markers
- [ ] Styrofoam cups
- [ ] cold beverages
- [ ] copies of handouts
- [ ] Bibles
- [ ] pencils

2. Vacuum-cleaner sales—
Divide the group into pairs. One person in each pair will be the vacuum-cleaner salesperson. The other person will be the customer. Have the salespeople try to sell vacuum cleaners to the customers. Then have the partners reverse roles.

Bring the whole group together to discuss these questions:
- What were the most effective sales methods?
- What turned off customers?
- What did the salespeople feel like?
- What did the customers feel like?

3. Cup of cold water—Ask, "What do you have to offer other people?" Give examples such as help with math, transportation, faith in God, friendship. Have each group member draw pictures on the outside of a Styrofoam cup of what he or she has to offer other people. After everyone has finished drawing, read Matthew 10:42. Have each group member show and explain his or her drawings. Serve cold drinks. Have kids save their cups.

4. "Living by the Sword"—Ask, "How do Christians sometimes turn off people when sharing their faith?" Form groups of four to six and give each person a copy of the "Living by the Sword" handout. Have kids discuss the questions in their groups.

5. Sharing match—Prepare enough "Sharing Your Faith Cards" from the handout so every group member can have one card. Distribute cards and have everyone stand in a circle. Direct each kid with a "Sharing Insight" card to find a kid with a matching "Sharing Verse" card. When all kids are matched in pairs, have each pair read their cards aloud and give one specific way to practice their sharing tips.

6. Report cards—Have each person complete the "Christian Report Card" handout. Discuss the grades.

7. Locker stickers—Have group members make locker stickers on small sheets of posterboard that tell about their faith in God but will not turn off other people.

8. Closing—Have the group sing "Go Tell It on the Mountain" or "Pass It On." For refreshments, serve refills of cold drinks.

Living by the Sword

Read the following scripture verse. Then answer the questions below.

"For the word of God is living and active. Sharper than any double-edged sword, it penetrates even to dividing soul and spirit, joints and marrow; it judges the thoughts and attitudes of the heart" (Hebrews 4:12).

What does this verse mean to you?

How can you apply it to the way you talk to people at school?

If Jesus stood beside you as you talked to some of your friends, what do you think he'd say?

Sharing Your Faith Cards

Photocopy and cut apart enough cards so each member of your group will have either a "Sharing Insight" or "Sharing Verse" card.

SHARING INSIGHT	SHARING VERSE
Ask for God's help. Realize that God has a plan for you and you can influence others for him.	"For I know the plans I have for you," declares the Lord, "plans to prosper you and not to harm you, plans to give you hope and a future" (Jeremiah 29:11).
Be a good friend. Help others as often as you can.	"A friend loves at all times, and a brother is born for adversity" (Proverbs 17:17).
Don't play favorites. Be kind to others without showing preferences.	"My brothers, as believers in our glorious Lord Jesus Christ, don't show favoritism" (James 2:1).
Keep a positive attitude. Be a conscientious student and a school leader.	"Your attitude should be the same as that of Christ Jesus" (Philippians 2:5).
Be diligent. Live a life that wins the respect of others.	"Make it your ambition to lead a quiet life, to mind your own business and to work with your hands, just as we told you, so that your daily life may win the respect of outsiders" (1 Thessalonians 4:11-12).
Don't give in to peer pressure. Stand up for what you know is right even when it seems everyone else is doing wrong. Escape temptation.	"No temptation has seized you except what is common to man. And God is faithful; he will not let you be tempted beyond what you can bear. But when you are tempted, he will also provide a way out so that you can stand up under it" (1 Corinthians 10:13).
Realize you're not better than others. Being a Christian doesn't make you a better person, just a forgiven one.	"For who makes you different from anyone else? What do you have that you did not receive? And if you did receive it, why do you boast as though you did not?" (1 Corinthians 4:7).

Christian Report Card

Grade yourself on how you represent Christ in your school. For each subject below, give yourself one of the following grades.

A: I'm doing well at this.
B: I'm doing okay, but I could do better.
C: Sometimes I do well, but other times I don't.
D: I'm weak in this area.
F: I need help.

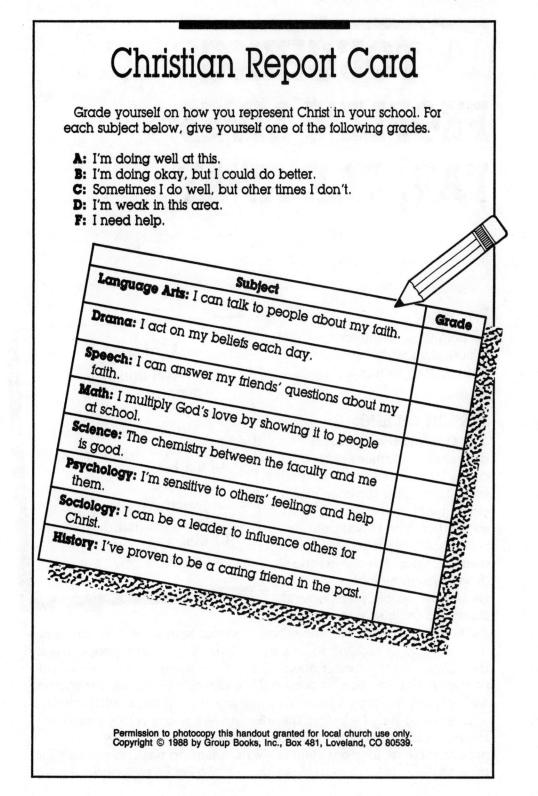

Subject	Grade
Language Arts: I can talk to people about my faith.	
Drama: I act on my beliefs each day.	
Speech: I can answer my friends' questions about my faith.	
Math: I multiply God's love by showing it to people at school.	
Science: The chemistry between the faculty and me is good.	
Psychology: I'm sensitive to others' feelings and help them.	
Sociology: I can be a leader to influence others for Christ.	
History: I've proven to be a caring friend in the past.	

14. TOUCHING PEOPLE'S LIVES FAR, FAR AWAY

Purpose:
To help group members put their concerns about hunger, poverty and missions to work.

Session outline:

1. One person makes a difference—Gather everyone in a circle. Have kids stand with their left sides toward the center of the circle, touching heel-to-toe with each other. The kids should be scrunched close together. On the count of three, have everyone sit down. Group members should land in the people's laps behind them; the circle should support

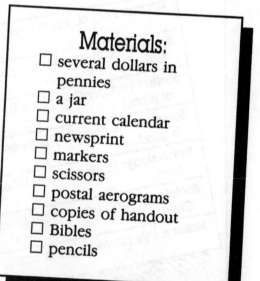

Materials:
- [ ] several dollars in pennies
- [ ] a jar
- [ ] current calendar
- [ ] newsprint
- [ ] markers
- [ ] scissors
- [ ] postal aerograms
- [ ] copies of handout
- [ ] Bibles
- [ ] pencils

itself. If one person falls, the whole circle collapses. Use this to point out the value of each person's contribution. Say: "Many people think they don't matter or can't make a difference when it comes to world problems. But one person does make a difference! During our meeting we'll explore what we can do to reach out in love to people far away."

2. Who to help?—Before the meeting, ask a few young people to research various missions projects. During the meeting, have them present three or four possibilities. Write them on newsprint. After the presentations, have the kids vote on one project to support in the coming months. Choose one person to be the contact who'll keep in touch with the project and provide information for the group.

3. Setting goals—Have kids read Matthew 25:31-46 aloud two or three times from different versions. Have a current calendar on hand. Have kids set deadlines and goals for their project. Include informational meetings and target amounts of money they plan to give.

4. "Fund Raisers"—Have kids each pick a partner. Give each pair a copy of one "Fund Raisers" idea clipped from the handout. If your group is smaller than 14, assign more than one idea to a pair. If your group is larger, repeat the assignments.

Tell each pair to read the idea together. Have one person argue against the idea, giving excuses and reasons why it would never work. Have the second person argue for the idea, telling why it would be great.

After a couple of minutes, have one pair for each idea present a one- to two-minute conversation for the entire group. After the presentations, have group members each choose one of the seven ideas to commit to for the duration of the project.

5. Letters of encouragement—Move kids into groups of four to six. Give each group a postal aerogram and have groups address the aerogram to the mission they have chosen to support. Have each small group member write a short paragraph in the letter. Tell kids to include in their paragraphs who they are, something about themselves and how they plan to earn money to support the project. Collect the sealed aerograms and mail them on your way home from the meeting. Repeat the letter-writing activity at least once each month during the project.

6. No refreshments—Give each group member a small handful of pennies. As you are handing them out, tell them that you are skipping refreshments for this meeting, and that the pennies they are receiving represent the money saved. Have them walk single-file to the front of the room and put their pennies in a jar. Say: "This money represents the beginning of our fund-raising project. Let's keep bringing our coins and bills each week until we reach our goal."

LOOK ON THE NEXT PAGE

Fund Raisers

Make several copies of these fund-raising ideas. Cut them apart and have them ready for use by pairs and individuals in the meeting.

● **Skip a meal regularly.**

Add the money you'd spend on a pizza or a burger to your goal. Or convince your family to eat one meatless meal each week and contribute the cost difference to your cause.

● **Take a part-time job.**

Your work can be doing chores around the house, cutting lawns, babysitting or delivering newspapers. Every time you're paid, dedicate part of the money to your missions project.

● **Fill a money jar.**

Find a unique jar to place in your room. Each evening, drop in the change from your pocket or purse. To celebrate a special occasion, toss in a roll of pennies.

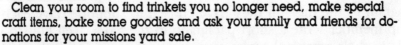

● **Hold a yard sale.**

Clean your room to find trinkets you no longer need, make special craft items, bake some goodies and ask your family and friends for donations for your missions yard sale.

● **Practice left pocket, right pocket money management.**

Keep your spending money in one pocket and your ministry money in the other. If you're a girl, use different purse compartments. Decide to put aside for missions a certain percentage of what you spend on yourself. When you buy something, move your pledge to your missions pocket.

● **Cut back on your spending.**

Write down everything you buy or spend money on in a two-week period. Carefully examine your spending habits. Pick an item or items that you can live without and reduce your spending. For example: Give up a movie a month or go to the bargain matinee.

● **Give up a soft drink a day.**

Set aside the money you save as you give up one or more soft drinks a day. A year's savings amounts to about $150.

15. WHEN PEOPLE IN YOUR GROUP COMPLAIN

Purpose:
To help group members learn how to understand and handle complainers.

Materials:
- ☐ masking tape
- ☐ paper or newsprint
- ☐ copies of handouts
- ☐ Bibles
- ☐ pencils
- ☐ refreshments

Session outline:

1. Getting ready—Create four squares on the meeting room floor with masking tape. Each square should be large enough for eight to 10 people to stand in. Label each square A, B, C or D.

2. "Favorite" squares—Get better acquainted. Designate each square with one of four answers to a question. Then, ask kids to each stand in the square that best represents their answer.

For example, ask: "What's your favorite season—winter, summer, spring or fall? Square A will represent winter, B will be summer, C will be spring and D will be fall."

After kids stand in the squares that represent their answers to a question, have them give reasons for their answers.

Ask other "favorite" questions like the following:

● What's your favorite color—red, yellow, blue or green?

● What's your favorite time of day—morning, afternoon, evening or late night?

● What's your favorite food—pizza, burgers, seafood or salad?

3. "Complaint department" squares—Tell the group the theme of this session is how to handle complainers.

Say: "You know the type. They can find something wrong with anything. They cast their shadow of negativism whenever they get the chance. They don't like the food. People aren't friendly. Youth group is boring. You never talk about God or you're too 'churchy.' The list goes on and on.

"We need to be prepared for complaints. Complainers like to voice their negative opinions, especially when they think you can do something about their gripe. You can't control what someone else says or does; however, you can control *your* response and reaction. Use this self-test to understand your attitude toward complainers."

Distribute the "How Do You Respond?" handout and have individuals circle their response to each situation.

Go through each situation in the self-quiz, and have group members stand in the squares that best represent their responses. After each situation, ask:

● What makes this situation hard to handle?

● Why would you react this way?

● Has something similar ever happened to you? If so, tell about it.

4. More to learn—Have group members form three groups. One group should be those who answered mostly A's; one, B's; and the other, C's. (If any group has more than eight members, divide it into smaller groups.)

Say: "What did you learn about yourself? Take a closer look at your attitudes. How do you typically respond?

"If you checked mostly A's, you avoid and ignore people who complain. You dismiss them whether or not they have something worthwhile to offer.

"If you checked mostly C's, you allow complainers to control you and make decisions for you. You let negative comments bring you down and you sometimes make irrational decisions based on one person's negative comments.

"If you checked mostly B's, you're secure. You choose to offer love, openness and forgiveness. You are willing to be the brunt of a lot of griping, yet you can't be pushed around by a few negative people. You are able to listen and act in love."

Encourage individuals to talk about their reactions to complainers and why they respond the way they do. Within the small groups have each person share an instance when he or she responded to complainers.

Have group "A" talk about:

● Why do I ignore complainers?

● What am I afraid of?

● How does my reaction affect the complainer?

Have group "B" discuss:

● Why do I handle complainers with confidence?

● How does a complainer feel when given a mature response?

● How can I improve?

Have group "C" ask:

● Why am I controlled by complainers?

● What is it that makes me want to change because of negative comments?

● What does my response tell complainers?

5. Helpful hints—Pass out "Hints for Handling Complainers" and read the directions with the group. Encourage individuals to share personal discoveries and other hints they might have.

6. "Love" squares—Label each floor square with one word: humbleness, gentleness, patience, tolerance. As a closing devotion, have kids stand in the square that says what they need most from people right now. Ask kids to look around them and pray for the people in their square.

Allow about a minute for silent prayer.

Next, have kids stand in the square that indicates the quality they need to give others—especially those who complain. Have kids look around them and pray for the people in their square.

Again allow about a minute for silent prayer.

Then have group members join hands, perhaps forming a square. Ask one young person to read Ephesians 4:1-2 as a final spoken prayer. Close by singing favorite "love" songs.

7. Snack squares—Serve refreshments that come in the shape of squares—cake, bars, brownies, pizza, crackers or other treats. For an added "love" touch, decorate the treats with hearts.

How Do You Respond?

Circle the letter that best represents how you'd respond in each situation.

1. Stan, a congregational member with a reputation for being negative, tells you the youth group isn't "spiritual" enough. You:
   a. pretend to listen, but dismiss Stan's complaint.
   b. listen intently, thank Stan for his thoughts and evaluate his comments later.
   c. immediately change your youth group programming to please him.
   d. other: _____

2. Betty, someone you respect and admire, says she thinks the youth group is falling apart. You:
   a. shrug your shoulders, sigh and say there's nothing you can do.
   b. work with her on ideas for improvement.
   c. feel hurt that someone you care about criticized your efforts.
   d. other: _____

3. Peggy, an inactive youth group member, tells you how much she dislikes the youth group activities and the people involved. You:
   a. feel angry and disagree with her. You wonder how she can say so since she never comes to youth group anyway.
   b. listen to what she's saying, and offer comments when appropriate. You don't necessarily agree with her, since she never comes to youth group meetings.
   c. agree and say, "Yes, the youth group's a mess."
   d. other: _____

4. The group clown, Sean, embarrasses you in front of the whole group with a personal putdown. You:
   a. act like you didn't hear him.
   b. repeat and reflect the meaning of what he said, so you can clarify his comment.
   c. get defensive and respond with a sarcastic comment.
   d. other: _____

5. Peter, Joel and Kim don't like the lights-out rule at the retreat. As usual, they're being uncooperative and complaining. You:
   a. tell them to shut up and obey the rules.
   b. restate the lights-out rule and give reasons why it's important.
   c. change lights-out time to please them even though they don't represent the whole group.
   d. other: _____

6. Jack, the church custodian, complains that the youth group doesn't clean up after its meetings. You:
   a. dismiss his complaint because he's too picky. Besides, you want to stick up for the group.
   b. admit mistakes and promise the group will improve.
   c. get depressed and give up.
   d. other: _____

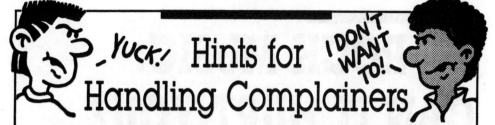

Hints for Handling Complainers

Read the following hints and think about how you might have applied these ideas in the past and how you might apply them in the future. Circle the hint you think will help you the most. List more hints below. Share your ideas with others in the group.

Use the following helpful suggestions for dealing with complainers:

● **Consider the source.** Try to understand where complainers are coming from. Remember some people choose to live in a negative cloud. When they're unhappy and dissatisfied with themselves, they take it out on others.

On the other hand, other complainers could be individuals with insight and valid concerns. You can recognize these complainers because they look for ways to improve the situation, not just tear it down.

● **Listen** to what a complainer is saying. Take some advice from James 1:19: "My dear brothers, take note of this: Everyone should be quick to listen, slow to speak and slow to become angry." Listen and reflect on what you hear the complainers saying. That doesn't mean you have to agree. It means you will listen to what they feel and say. In many situations, *you* know the total picture and they don't. Often after they've unloaded their complaint, they're satisfied. Some people just need to complain.

● **Remain calm** and don't get defensive. Sometimes gripers enjoy getting a reaction, especially out of a leader. It's one way they can feel in control. When they get a response from you, they've accomplished their purpose. Surprise them. Don't raise your voice or defend yourself. Simply say: "I hear what you're saying. Thank you for letting me know how you feel."

● **Restate your reasons.** People sometimes complain about guidelines that are meant to benefit the whole group. They don't like the rules. Continue to rephrase and restate the reasoning. Be firm and say, "This is how it is." When you can use others to back the guideline or rule, do so. For example, remind complainers that the youth council, parents or the entire youth group set the rule and you're just helping to enforce it for them.

● **Be willing to bend** if the complainer has a valid point. You will gain great respect if you're willing to risk, make mistakes and accept responsibility for improvements. A sign of strength is an ability to be flexible when necessary.

● **Let love guide you.** "Be patient, bearing with one another in love" (Ephesians 4:2). Patience, tolerance and love tell others you think they are valuable, even when you don't particularly like the person or what a complainer says. God's love shining through you will help you cope with the most difficult of complainers. So shine on!

● **Other hints:**

16. ROCK MUSIC: CAN IT HURT YOU?

Purpose:
To help group members evaluate the kinds of music they listen to.

Session outline:

1. Before the meeting—Ask kids to bring albums, posters, T-shirts or other items that reflect their favorite music.

2. Musical mood—As kids arrive, play contemporary Christian music on a good sound system. Designate one area for kids to tape up or display their favorite albums, posters, T-shirts, whatever.

3. A letter—Play some soft background music from one of the albums that the kids brought as you read the following letter. Tell the kids that Dennis Benson is the dad who wrote this letter. He's a Christian who's interviewed hundreds of rock stars.

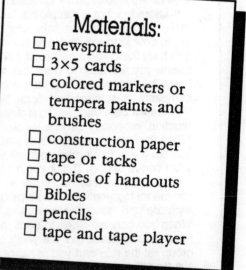

Materials:
- [ ] newsprint
- [ ] 3×5 cards
- [ ] colored markers or tempera paints and brushes
- [ ] construction paper
- [ ] tape or tacks
- [ ] copies of handouts
- [ ] Bibles
- [ ] pencils
- [ ] tape and tape player

> *Dear Jill and Amy,*
> *I can hardly believe my two little girls have become dazzling teenagers. And now you're young adults with a range of personal decisions beyond my fatherly participation or direct advice.*
> *I can't always watch you experience movies, rock songs and other cultural bits of influence and entertainment. So I*

wonder. Does the casual morality of a song influence your moral decisions? Because all three of us like a "love" song, will you think sex without love and commitment is acceptable?

These crazy flashes of worry must seem strange coming from your father. You know I love rock 'n roll. You've even gone with me on my visits to interview rock stars. You were only four and seven when a rock star took you on a back-stage tour and got you both Cokes and ice cream cones!

Fathers want to protect their kids from the bad and evil. But you no longer want and need someone to make moral decisions for you. Now you're responsible young women.

You'll discover good and evil surround you each moment of every day. And the only basis for judging truth comes from what God in Jesus Christ puts into your life. Today's wicked rock song or immoral soap opera will be replaced by another example of temptation tomorrow. What remains constant is the living power of Christ inside you. This source will never fail you.

May God continue to bless you with the courage to listen to the truth and the strength to live it.

Peace, Dad

Discuss the following questions with the whole group:

● Would your mom or dad write you a letter like this? Why or why not?

● Do you agree that teenagers no longer "want and need someone to make moral decisions" for them? Why or why not?

● What people in your life try to make decisions for you? Why?

● Why does the dad say "today's wicked rock song or immoral soap opera will be replaced by another example of temptation tomorrow"?

● After receiving this letter, should Jill and Amy listen to rock music? Why or why not?

● Should you? Why or why not?

4. "The Great Debate"—Give everyone a copy of "The Great Debate" handout. Divide the kids into two groups and designate one group "Pros" and the other "Cons." Have each group discuss its list and brainstorm more "Pros" or "Cons" to rock music. Have each group select one representative to give a two-minute argument for its position to the whole group. After the debate, have kids vote by applauding and cheering for the side that was most convincing.

5. Who's your favorite?—Give each group member a copy of the "Rock Star Interviews" handout and have everyone complete Part 1 of the handout individually as instructed. Play some background music as kids work. Have kids pair up to share answers. Then have pairs complete Part 2 together.

6. "Top 10"—Bring the kids back together as a large group. Ask kids to suggest five current top songs in contemporary Christian music and five in secular music. List song titles on two separate sheets of newsprint labeled "Christian" and "Secular."

Give kids copies of the "Top 10" handout and have them complete the exercise individually using the song titles listed on the newsprint. Have volunteers share their responses with the whole group.

7. The sounds of scripture—Give each group member a 3×5 card. Assign seven kids to read the following scripture passages: Deuteronomy 6:5-9; Psalm 150; Romans 12:1-2, 9; Galatians 5:19-25; Ephesians 5:1-2,19; Philippians 4:8; Colossians 3:16-17. After each passage has been read, ask kids to write on their cards the passage reference and what God is telling them through that passage.

8. What do you say?—Tell kids that they are being interviewed by a popular magazine for teenagers. Ask, "How would you like to be quoted in the magazine concerning your opinion about rock music?" Have them write their quotes on the back of their 3×5 cards. Ask several to share what they wrote.

9. A musical prayer—Have a young person choose one contemporary Christian song as a closing prayer. Give kids construction paper and colored markers (or bright tempera paints and brushes). Play the song and have kids "draw" the song as they listen. Hang the prayer posters on the meeting room wall.

The Great Debate

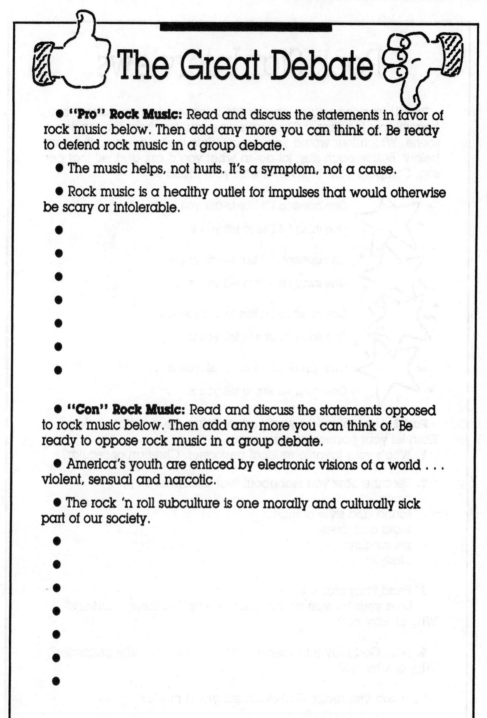

- **"Pro" Rock Music:** Read and discuss the statements in favor of rock music below. Then add any more you can think of. Be ready to defend rock music in a group debate.

- The music helps, not hurts. It's a symptom, not a cause.

- Rock music is a healthy outlet for impulses that would otherwise be scary or intolerable.

-
-
-
-
-
-

- **"Con" Rock Music:** Read and discuss the statements opposed to rock music below. Then add any more you can think of. Be ready to oppose rock music in a group debate.

- America's youth are enticed by electronic visions of a world . . . violent, sensual and narcotic.

- The rock 'n roll subculture is one morally and culturally sick part of our society.

-
-
-
-
-
-

Rock Star Interviews

Part 1: Imagine you're assigned to interview four musicians—two from the contemporary Christian scene and two from the secular scene. Which four would you select? Write their names on the stars below. Beside each star, jot down what you'd ask and tell that person. Compare your interviews with your friend's.

One question I'd like to ask you is . . .

One thing I'd like to tell you is . . .

One question I'd like to ask you is . . .

One thing I'd like to tell you is . . .

One question I'd like to ask you is . . .

One thing I'd like to tell you is . . .

One question I'd like to ask you is . . .

One thing I'd like to tell you is . . .

Part 2: Now interview your partner using the questions below. Then let your partner interview you.

1. Who's your favorite musical performer, Christian or secular?

2. Describe how you feel about that performer's . . .
lyrics:
sound and style of music:
looks and dress:
personality:
lifestyle:

3. Read Philippians 4:8.
Does your favorite group "measure up" to these standards? Why or why not?

4. Does God play into your decision about a favorite performer? Why or why not?

How can you make God-decisions about music?

☆Top 10☆

Write the titles to your group's top 10 songs in the spaces below. Use the following code to evaluate each musical hit. Place the appropriate symbol or letters that apply in the boxes beside each song—according to your opinion. Then talk about your ratings.

The code:
B—It has a good beat.
L—It has good lyrics.
M—I can relate to the message.
P—It gives a positive view of life.
N—It gives a negative view of life.
$—I'd buy it!

Top songs in contemporary Christian music:

1. _____

2. _____

3. _____

4. _____

5. _____

Top songs in secular music:

1. _____

2. _____

3. _____

4. _____

5. _____

17. AIDS

Purpose:

To help group members discuss their thoughts about AIDS and see how labels determine how we treat people.

Session outline:

1. Labels—Ask each group member to bring a can of soup to the meeting. Give each person a piece of paper and a pencil. Have kids list everything the soup-can labels tell consumers. For example, what's in the can, nutritional value and manufacturer. Then compare can labels to people labels. Have group members list kids' labels in school such as jock, beautiful person, egghead, nerd, and one who's part of the "in" crowd. Ask, "How do kids treat people with these labels?"

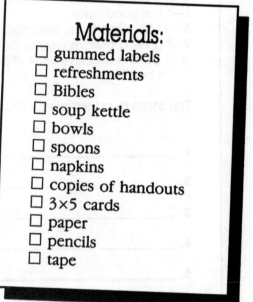

Materials:

- ☐ gummed labels
- ☐ refreshments
- ☐ Bibles
- ☐ soup kettle
- ☐ bowls
- ☐ spoons
- ☐ napkins
- ☐ copies of handouts
- ☐ 3×5 cards
- ☐ paper
- ☐ pencils
- ☐ tape

2. Let's have a party—Place a gummed label on each person's forehead. Write on the labels descriptive words such as "beautiful," "rich," "poor," "ugly," "athletic," "stuck-up," "funny," "homosexual," "AIDS victim," "smart" and "dumb." Don't tell kids what label they're wearing. Tell kids to treat each other as if they're really like the labels they're wearing. Play party games for 30 minutes.

Ask: "How did you feel during the party? ignored? favored?" Have kids guess their labels, then remove them from their foreheads. Ask: "How did your label determine how others treated you? How did labels determine how you treated them?"

Read Matthew 7:1-5 and talk about how easily we label and see faults (or "logs") in other people, even though we may have bigger faults ourselves. (During this discussion, serve celery pieces or "logs" with the center filled with peanut butter.)

3. "Agree/Disagree"—Pass out "Agree/Disagree." Tell the group: "One label that causes people to react in fear and misunderstanding is AIDS. When an individual is labeled as an AIDS victim, he or she experiences a prejudice that limits or alters interaction with the rest of society. For example, look at the handout." Ask young people to read each statement and mark each continuum according to how they feel about the statement. Discuss responses.

4. "What Does God Say?"—Pass out the "What Does God Say?" cards to individuals or small groups. Ask them to read the scripture passages and be prepared to report their findings to the total group. After each report, ask, "What does God say about labeling others in this passage?"

5. "What's Fair?"—Have group members each fill out the "What's Fair?" chart. Discuss answers.

6. New skits—Form groups of four to six. Tell half the groups to read Matthew 8:1-4 and the other half to read Luke 17:11-19. Have each group write a skit placing its Bible story in a modern setting. Present the skits.

7. Positive labels—Have kids get back in groups of four to six. Give group members each enough gummed labels so they can give a label to every person (besides themselves) in their group. Ask each person to write on separate labels a positive quality for every person in the group. Have kids place the labels on the foreheads of the appropriate people. Then have them walk around reading each other's labels. Encourage hugs.

8. Hobo stew—Pour the soup-cans' contents into a kettle. Heat and serve "hobo stew."

TURN THE PAGE!

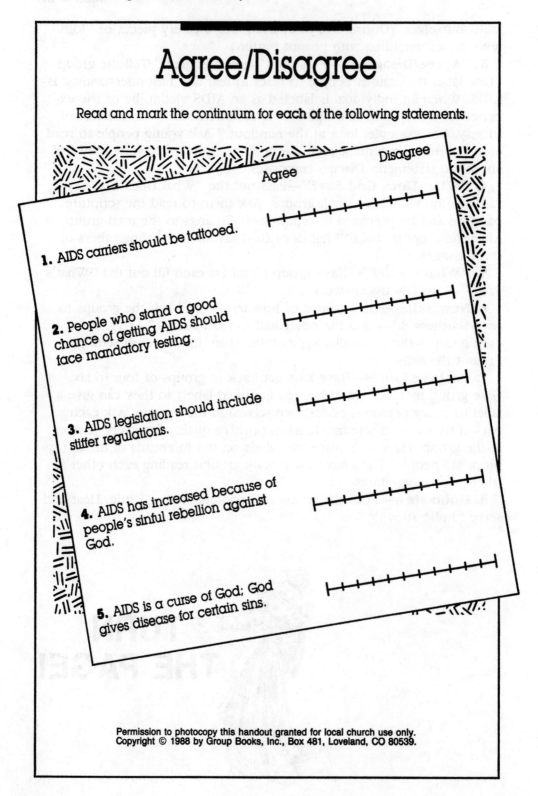

Agree/Disagree

Read and mark the continuum for **each** of the following statements.

Agree · · · · · · · · · · Disagree

1. AIDS carriers should be tattooed.

2. People who stand a good chance of getting AIDS should face mandatory testing.

3. AIDS legislation should include stiffer regulations.

4. AIDS has increased because of people's sinful rebellion against God.

5. AIDS is a curse of God; God gives disease for certain sins.

What Does God Say?

Copy this page and cut it apart. Tape each scripture passage with its questions to a 3×5 card.

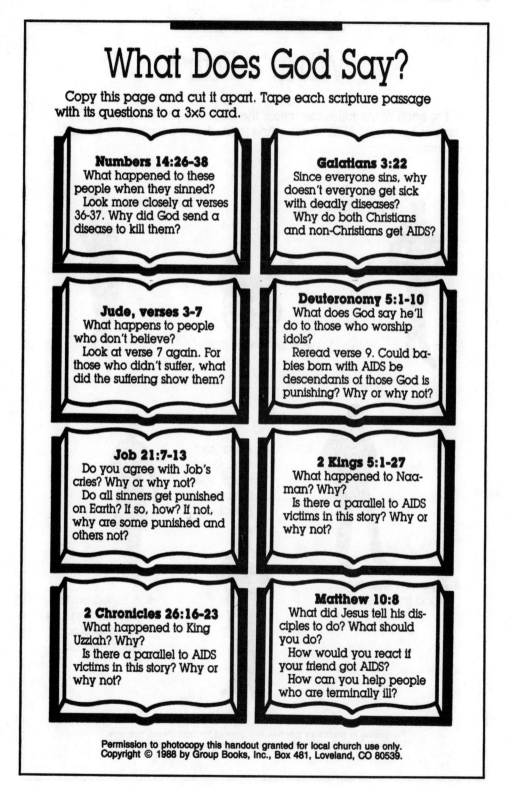

Numbers 14:26-38
What happened to these people when they sinned?
Look more closely at verses 36-37. Why did God send a disease to kill them?

Galatians 3:22
Since everyone sins, why doesn't everyone get sick with deadly diseases?
Why do both Christians and non-Christians get AIDS?

Jude, verses 3-7
What happens to people who don't believe?
Look at verse 7 again. For those who didn't suffer, what did the suffering show them?

Deuteronomy 5:1-10
What does God say he'll do to those who worship idols?
Reread verse 9. Could babies born with AIDS be descendants of those God is punishing? Why or why not?

Job 21:7-13
Do you agree with Job's cries? Why or why not?
Do all sinners get punished on Earth? If so, how? If not, why are some punished and others not?

2 Kings 5:1-27
What happened to Naaman? Why?
Is there a parallel to AIDS victims in this story? Why or why not?

2 Chronicles 26:16-23
What happened to King Uzziah? Why?
Is there a parallel to AIDS victims in this story? Why or why not?

Matthew 10:8
What did Jesus tell his disciples to do? What should you do?
How would you react if your friend got AIDS?
How can you help people who are terminally ill?

What's Fair?

For each of the following, circle the person if you think it's fair for him or her to get AIDS; draw a line through the person if it's unfair. Explain.

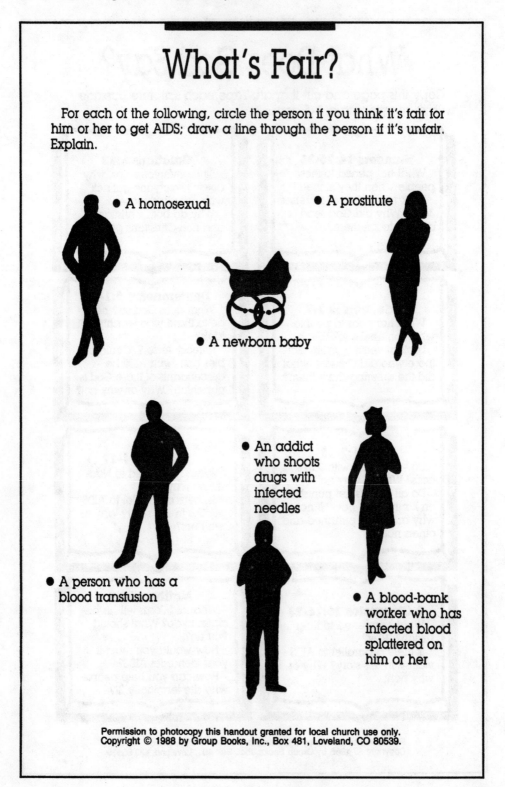

● A homosexual

● A prostitute

● A newborn baby

● An addict who shoots drugs with infected needles

● A person who has a blood transfusion

● A blood-bank worker who has infected blood splattered on him or her